For more information or to book an event, please contact: elioendleeshouse@gmail.com

Book design by Kai

Cover design by Tyson

Paperback ISBN:

ebook ISBN:

"A RESEARCH OF MONEY THE CONTROL AND THE BANKING HABITS AMONG THE HOSTELITE

ELIO ENDLESS PUBLISHERS

To Dad, Mom, and my supportive colleagues,Your love, guidance, and unwavering support have been the driving force behind my journey as a writer. Thank you for believing in me and encouraging me to pursue my dreams. Your presence in my life has made all the difference.
With heartfelt gratitude,
ELIO.E

Preface

Hey there, "wave"! How's it going? I'm your friendly neighborhood book editor, here to tell you about this amazing book that just landed on our shelves. It's a gem that our awesome publishing company has brought to life. Now, as part of my job, I get to dive into countless books, and I must say, this one is an absolute delight. No need for any unnecessary delay, let me give you a sneak peek into what makes it so worthwhile. Are you ready? Let's jump right in with the introduction. An activity that refers to the process through which a bank, which is an entity that deals with financial transactions, commercial a bank belonging to either the public or the private sector, banking is an activity that refers to the process by which a bank engages with customers. It is a place of business that offers the following services and more:the provision of a number of different financial services, one of which is the lending of money, among other financial services. transactions involving credit cards and debit cards, as well as the collection of deposits and the issue of money, are all included. systems such as transaction processing, among others, are the very last but certainly not the least.The "Banking Company" that is referred to in the Indian Banking Regulation Act of 1949 is actually a reference to an institution.It is accountable for the day-to-day activities and operations of the banking sector in India. Passage of the Banking Act, Section 5(b), and the Regulation Act of 1949 took place. A firm that accepts deposits from customers is referred to as banking. The rationale for lending money or the amount of money that is lent for investment is also referred to as banking. It is probable that these are deposits of money made by members of the general public, money that must be paid back to these individuals on their demand or else, and withdrawals made by means of cheques, drafts, money orders, or any other method. The defining moment in historical context, when The year 1969 was pivotal in the annals of banking history in India because that was the year that 14 of the country's most important banks were taken over by the government.whereas in the 1980s additional banks went on to form what is now what constitutes the public sector, the public sectorector banks, the public sector banks today constitute the public sector.Banks in the modern period have expanded their operations well beyond the daily tasks that were typical of them in the past.business that consists exclusively of taking deposits and, in exchange for the money, lends it to a range of various segments of society that are either more privileged or weaker than other portions. Both urban and rural banking in India have witnessed substantial alterations as a result of the introduction of contemporary technology.to a rural extent, the presentation of a number of creative andto a rural extent, the introduction of modern technologies. It has been deployed in a wide variety of industries and distribution channels, including debit card transactions, for instance, or other payment methods such as credit cards, core banking solutions, internet banking, mobile banking, or telebanking, etc. One of the most important objectives of the business, which is a developing corporate body, is to reduce the amount of borrowing it does.banks.

Now that things have progressed to this stage, banks are mandated to put more of their attention on the concept of retail banking. MostBanks have made increasing their lending of money for personal financial matters a key focus of their operations, and as a result, they have become more active in this sector.finance for individuals or for small businesses. financing of homes and the education industry as a whole are both areas of focus. In addition, we are making an effort to study a range of prospective channels for the generation of profits for the banks, and we are looking into a variety of potential paths.PQE for the SI unitsThe vast majority of the nation's financial institutions are structured as businesses with the primary goal of making a profit for their owners. Whatever the situation. There are only a handful of government banks that carry out their business operations as separate legal entities from charitable organizations.Generally speaking, the government agencies, which may also be referred to as central banks or government banks, are the ones who are in charge ofThe movement and circulation of money should also be regulated, in addition to the various interest rates. This should be the primary focus of attention.in terms of the economy of the nation of the Ln Clian.As a direct consequence of this, there is an urgent imperative to put into action a strategy that is both all-encompassing and well-organized in order to cultivate a culture of frugality and appropriate banking practices among individuals of all demographics... The routine of banking, which has now become a routine, needs to be instilled, nurtured, and developed to its maximum capacity in order to be successful.beginning immediately at the beginning of their childhoods1.2 Creating a Budget and Planning Your Finances:The process of taking charge of one's financial situation is *known as "money management," and it entails a series of actions on the part of the individual in question. one's monetary affairs, financial planning, financial management, and tax preparation, among other related topics. Additionally, it is referred to as a subfield inside the investment sector.the administration. The process of controlling one's own financial resources also goes by the name of budgeting, which is another term that can be used to refer to the activity.expenses that were made. putting money aside, making investments, keeping an eye on it, or putting it to some other use with the cashfrom the perspective of an individual or a group.By utilizing a tactical approach known as money management, an individual is able to enhance their current state of financial well-being.money provide him the highest return on investment in terms of interest yielded or retum value for the amount that was spent or value that was spent. money give him the most return on investment. The concept or idea of financial management, as well as its numerous forms and methods, have been conceived of or developed in order to reduce the amount of what individuals, businesses, and governments need to spend their time and energy doing.The aggregate sum of money that a number of small and medium-sized enterprises as well as other institutions spend on a variety of goodsvalue that is either little to the companies or significant to the individuals in terms of the living standards it affects. lengthy period of timeportfolios and the assets under management in such portfolios. Warren Buffett, widely regarded as one of the most successful and smart investors in the world, has advised prospective and regular investors to watch one of their documentaries, all of which are available on their website and may be accessed there.embrace as your own and instill in others his highly renowned and self-proclaimed "frugality" philosophy. accept as your own and instill in others.The concept of "frugality" refers to the practice of trying to get* the most value out of every single dollar, regardless of whether it was earned or spent.transaction in the field of finance that was more than worth the price:I. Stay away from any kind of expenditure, no matter how trivial or inconsequential it may seem, that caters to your tum's vanity or elitism.I am currently on page 6).2. Make your decision based on whatever alternative will end up saving you the most money overall. Looking for relatively insignificant variances and benchmarks, if there are any that are required.3. Devote a greater portion of your income to investments that generate interest and put these investments ahead of all others in terms of importance.expenses that were made.

Personal finances of the individual:The administration of a person's or family's financial resources is what's meant to be referred to when using the word "personal finance."whatever it is that needs to be done in order to acquire, arrange one's finances, put money aside, and spend money on a variety of resources over the course of the length of time, taking into account the numerous financial hazards.and the prospective life events that may take place in the future.1.4 A condensed explanation of the problem is as follows:Many students in higher education are on the verge of falling into financial hardship, and a significant number of them actually do fall into that category.not be in possession of the knowledge required to effectively handle their finances in the appropriate manner. Attend lectures at one of the colleges while the students were seated at their desks. They are continually accumulating more debt as a result of their continued engagement in new borrowing.the majority of the funds came from personal credit cards and loans for students. It's possible that they won't realize how their current debt could potentially affect their future in a way that is unfavorable or adverse to them right now, but it doesn't mean they won't eventually come to that realization.the credit rating, *in addition to the budget for both savings and consumption. In the absence of rigorous and consistent financial regulationsStudents will have a tough time reaching their full potential if they incorporate managerial methods into both their short-term and long-term monetary goals in their practices.This study aimed to analyze the academic experiences of bow students who were enrolled in programs leading to undergraduate degrees or postgraduate degrees that taught students how to effectively manage their financial resources. The information was gleaned from the students' own records of their income and expenditures throughout the course of the academic year.Individual interviews were carried out over the course of a period of time spanning a span of two years. This research project is referred to asdeveloped with the intention of getting a more comprehensive and quantitative understanding of the financial andbehavior of college students during their undergraduate and graduate years from the point of view of financial classes delivered at a large institution.As a direct consequence of this, there is an urgent necessity to do research into the procedures of money management and banking.*

Acknowledgements

I would like to take this opportunity to extend my heartfelt thanks to all the individuals who have played a significant role in the creation of this non-fiction book. Your unwavering support, valuable advice, and constant encouragement have been invaluable throughout this journey. I am deeply grateful to those who have provided me with aspirational direction, constructive criticism, and kind advice. Your feedback has been instrumental in shaping the content and direction of this book. I genuinely appreciate your candid insights into my project.I am particularly grateful for the exceptional assistance of Mr. Jaffer and Mrs. Sameena at Endless Publishers. Their continuous support, dedication, and guidance have been instrumental in helping me overcome obstacles and improve the quality of my work. I am sincerely appreciative of their tremendous efforts and unwavering belief in this project.I would also like to express my heartfelt appreciation to Mr. Ahmed, my project's external advisor from Ahmed Corporation. His invaluable advice, insightful critique, and vast wisdom have played a pivotal role in refining my thoughts and enhancing the overall quality of this book. I am truly grateful for his guidance and expertise. Furthermore, I would like to acknowledge Ms. Sultana and every individual who has contributed to obtaining the necessary resources and making this initiative possible. Your assistance, whether it was in sourcing information, conducting research, or providing logistical support, is deeply appreciated. This book would not have come to fruition without your invaluable contributions. I cannot overlook the individual who initially sparked the flame of inspiration within me to embark on this book-writing endeavor. Your unwavering belief in my abilities, continuous motivation, and unending support throughout this artistic process have been instrumental in my journey. I am forever indebted to you for being my constant source of inspiration. I want to express my deepest gratitude to every person who has contributed to this project, no matter how small their role may have been. Each and every one of you has played a part in making this book possible, and your contributions have not gone unnoticed. Your support, encouragement, and assistance have been instrumental in bringing this book to fruition. Finally, I would like to give special credit to Kai, B.EE, and Tyson, the pen names that have accompanied me on this writing adventure. Your creativity, distinct perspectives, and unique insights have added depth and character to this book. I am honored to have had the opportunity to collaborate with you. To all of you who have been a part of this remarkable journey, I extend my deepest gratitude. Your unwavering support, guidance, and friendship have been invaluable. Thank you for believing in me and for contributing to the realization of this non-fiction book. With

sincere appreciation,

Elio Endless

EDITOR NOTE

1. Publisher Notes: This edition is a product of inspiration from other works, with a portion of its content derived from public domain sources. Elioendless, the creator, editor, and publisher of the ebook edition, utilized manuscripts, select texts, and illustrative images from public domain archives. Members can acquire this ebook from our website for personal use. However, please note that any form of commercial storage, transmission, or reverse engineering of this file is strictly prohibited.

Contents

CHAPTER ONE

borrowing banks

B anking is an activity that refers to the process through which a bank, which is an institution that deals with financial transactions,commercial a bank belonging to either the public or the private sector. It is an establishment that provides the following:the provision of a variety of financial services, some of which include the lending of money. gathering updeposits, the issuance of currency, as well as credit and debit card transactions. the last but not leastsystems such as transaction processing etc.An institution is what the Indian Banking Regulation Act of 1949 refers to when it says "Banking Company."It is responsible for the day-to-day operations and activities of banking in India. The Banking Act, Section 5(b),1949's Regulation Act was passed. definition of banking as a business that accepts deposits from customersreason for lending money or the quantity of money lent for investment. It is possible that these are deposits of money.from members of the general public, money that must be paid back on their demand or else, and thewithdrawals made through checks, drafts, money orders, or in any other fashion. The pivotal point in history whenThe year 1969 is significant in the history of banking in India since it was the year that 14 major banks were nationalized.whereas in the 1980s more banks were joined on to construct what now constitutes the public sector, the public sectorsector banks.The banks of the modern era have broadened their operations beyond the typical daily activities.activity consisting solely of taking deposits and, in exchange, lending money to a variety of differentparts of society that are either privileged or weaker than others. The presentation of a number of innovative andBoth urban and rural banking in India have seen significant transformations as a result of the introduction of modern technologies.to a rural extent. It has been implemented in a variety of domains and channels, including debit card transactions, for example.or other payment methods such as credit cards, core banking solutions, internet banking, mobile banking, or telebanking .etc. As a growing corporate entity, one of the corporation's primary goals is to decrease its level of borrowing.banks.

It has gotten to the point that banks are even required to concentrate on the idea of retail banking. MostThe lending of money for personal finances has been a primary priority for banks, and these institutions have become more aggressive in this area.consumer or small business financing. housing finance, as well as the education sector as a whole. The banks areadditionally, we are making an effort to investigate a variety of potential avenues for the generation of the profits.SI Units: pqeThe bulk of financial institutions in the country are organized as for-profit businesses. In any case. aThere are only a very small number, or very few, government banks that operate as entities of non-profit organizations.The government agencies, sometimes known as central banks or govement banks, are the ones who typicallyAttention should be focused on regulating the various interest rates as well as the movement and circulation of money.in the economics of the ln clian nation.As a result, there is a pressing requirement to implement a comprehensive and organized strategy forfostering a culture of thrift and responsible banking practices among people of all demographics... The The routine of banking. having become a routine. has to be imbued, nourished, and developed to its full potential.right from the start of their childhoods1.2 Budgeting and Financial Planning:The practice of managing one's financial resources is referred to as "money management," and it includes a number of steps. one·smonetary matters, financial planning, financial management, and tax preparation. It is also known as a subfield of the investing industry.the management. Budgeting is another term that can be used to refer to the practice of managing one's finances.costs incurred. putting money aside, making investments, overseeing it, or putting it to some other use with the cashan individual's or a group's point of view.One can improve their financial situation by the application of a strategic method known as money management.money give him the greatest return on investment in terms of interest yielded or retum value for the amount that was spent orvalue that was spent. The notion or idea of financial management, as well as its various formsmethods have been conceived of or developed in order to cut down on the quantity of what individuals,The total amount that several small and medium-sized businesses and institutions spend on various productsvalue that is either little or significant to the firms and individuals in terms of their living standards. lengthy durationportfolios and the assets that were managed. Warren Buffett, one of the world's most successful and astute investors, hadhas cautioned potential and regular investors to watch one of their documentaries, which may be accessed on their website.accept as your own and instill in others his highly regarded and self-proclaimed "frugality" worldview.This philosophy of "frugality" entails maximizing the return on each and every one of one's dollars spent or earned.transaction in finance that was well worth the cost:I. Avoid any form of expense, no matter how modest or iliat, that appeals to your tum into vanity or snobbery.I am on page 6)2. Choose the option that will save you the most money at all times. Looking for quite minor differences andbenchmarks, if there are any necessary.3. Spend more on interest-bearing investments than you take in, and prioritize these investments over all others.costs incurred.

Finances de la personne:The term "personal finance" refers to the management of an individual's or family's financial resources.whatever must be done in order to acquire, organize one's finances, put money away, and spend money of a varietyresources over the course of the length of time, taking into account the numerous financial hazards.and the potential life events that may take place in the future.1.4 A brief description of the issue:Many college students are teetering on the brink of a financial crisis, and many of them really fall into that category.not be in possession of the knowledge necessary to properly handle their finances. As pupils sat at their desks,attend classes at one of the colleges. They are continuously adding to their debt by engaging in additional borrowing.mostly through personal credit cards and student loans. It's possible at this moment that they won't.recognize how their current debt will potentially effect their future in a way that is detrimental or unfavorable to themThe credit rating, as well as the savings and spending panem. In the absence of stringent and consistent monetaryStudents will have a difficult time reaching their potential when they apply managerial practices in their practices.their

4

immediate as well as their long-term monetary objectives.The goal of this study was to investigate the academic experiences of bow students who were enrolled in undergraduate programs.and advanced degrees that teach students how to manage their financial resources. The data wereobtained from the student records of their expenditures as well as their income during the course of the yearindividual interviews conducted over the course of a two-year period's worth of time. This study is referred to asdeveloped with the goal of acquiring a more complete and quantitative understanding of the financial andbehavior of college students in their undergraduate and graduate years from a financial perspectiveclasses offered at a significant.As a result, there is a pressing requirement to investigate the practices of money management and banking.

Hoste light students make up this group.7 years of age1.5 Personal Banking Practices:According to the findings of the research, one of the problems that are caused by the programming is the cultivation andThe formation of banking routines among hostelite college students enrolled in tmdcrgraduate programsas well as courses for postgraduates. The financial practices, which constitute both its definition and its meaning.refers to the process of making efficient use of financial institutions like banks. In accordance with J. The Oljih Banking SystemThe degree to which individuals in a particular state are willing and eager to engage in a particular behavior is known as their habit.economy to make use of the various banking services and to make economic sense of them. Therefore, theThe researcher felt the need to find out whether or not the pupils were aware of any of the topics he was studying.Many Products and Services Offered by Banks? Did they instill the routine of Income and Expenditure?Expenditure from the perspective of Savings, and so on and so forth. Having this in mind thus. the study consisted ofIndividuals enrolled in undergraduate and postgraduate programs are required to take this specific course.The city of pune.To be more specific. This study and that research were carried out so that we might investigate the following:investigate the following questions and learn more about them:I. How do students who come from economically disadvantaged backgrounds handle their college finances?:!. What exactly is the topic of "Money and the Financial Management Behaviors of Hostelite Students"?.

What are the differences in the ways those who work and those who don't work manage their money?students, yes?4. What exactly is the nature of the gambling habit that is so prevalent among college students?1.6 The importance of the studyCollege students need to be educated about the importance of saving money and taught how to make it a habit.straight from their tender and impressionable years. That stage of life consists of graduate and postgraduate study.where the vast majority of kids are absent!Stay with their parents and choose between staying in a hostel or in aFlat or on a Sharing Basis Both Available.They are given a certain amount of money, which they are tasked with managing appropriately.c osts incurred for approximately one month until the subsequent payment is credited. Taking into consideration the normof being alive. The pattern of spending and the costs of living are frequently the same. The amount of... soThe amount that was received is insufficient to be managed for a particular period of time. Certain students fall under this category.w ho are not provided with an adequate quantity of financial support by their parents. Therefore, a few of themmust engage in (part-time) paid labor. Some of them get student loans, while others even get jobs and continue their studies.attend classes at multiple colleges at the same time.

Here is when a student in faces the challenge in monetary administration, including an explanation of the difference between spending and putting money away. The majority of the time, as this gap begins to widen, they shift their focus to Credit and begin to looking into a variety of possibilities that might provide a solution to their problem for the time being. May it be with the assistance of a friend. roommate, colleague, and teachers all come to mind. the likes of banks etc. Having insight into This subject has been selected by the researcher who is conducting the study regarding the pupils' expertise. concerning their typical method of expenditure as well as the extent of their financial literacy. 1. 7 A Selected Review of the Related Previous Research on the Subject The Indian Institute of Banking & Finance's publication on "Banking products and services" it helps students better understand both the theory and practice of banking and finance. It explains it in detail. the development of banking, as well as its various aspects and divisions. In addition to that, it discusses the many several kinds of deposits and financial accounts. products and services related to banking.

monetary, retail advances banking, wealth management, and other related fields. ("'Banking Products and Services... by the Indian Institute of Banking and Finance. Taxmann presents lecture notes written by Ms. Chitra Andrade, a marketing and tax professional. Printed Materials) B. According to the findings presented by Ragbavendra Rau in his study work titled "The Banking Habit in India," the conclusion was drawn that the tendency of hoarding should be eradicated, and that the habit of bailing should be increased. deep roots in the soil of Lnruan. For this reason, a few prudent banking considerations and procedures should be taken. It is recommended that the branch banking policy be pursued, as well as the Hindu Law of Inheritance.should be changed so that it is possible for a parent to distribute his possessions equally among his children.confidence in banks and banking should be encouraged in children of all ages, particularly sons and daughters.The Reserve Bank of India ought to expand its facilities and the facilities it provides for investments.according to what Raghavendra has said.(The Banking Habit in Thailand by Raghavendra Rau, taken from the website:The following article can be found at: http:/www.yabaluri.org/TRfVENVCDWEBffhcBankingHabitinlndiamay39.htm)The Institute of Chartered Financial Analysts published "Banking in the New Millennium" in 1999.Analysts from CF A of India (ICF AI) are concentrating their efforts on the company's newly developed areas.the incorporation of new forms of technology and forms of communication inside the banking industry.addresses the many obstacles that retail banking institutions must overcome in order to keep their consumers.the consolidation of private sector banks with their equivalent peer banks in order to compete with large and well-established banksIt also includes an essay on "Universal Banking," which refers to the previously-established public sector banks.can radically alter the way banking is done across India as a whole.The Institute of Chartered Financial Analysts presents "Banking in the New Millennium."

The press)The use of credit cards by students at colleges and universities, Charles Blankson and AudheshAll of them work in the Department of Marketing and Logistics and their names are Paswao Kwabena G. Boakye .University of North Texas, located in Denton, Texas, in the United States of America. The significance of and potential forThe college student demographic for financial institutions like credit card companies and banks is well recognized, and as a resultare the hurdles that businesses with an interest in targeting this market must face. The primary objective of this paper was to investigate the factors that drive college students to succeed academically. using credit cards and making the most of the benefits those cards provide for them is the second objective. depended on the guidance of marketing researchers by first reproducing, and then confirming, an existing scale. that analyzes the factors that influence college students' choices regarding credit cards, in particular, thestudy made an attempt to answer two questions: what is the compelling rationale for a college education, and what are the benefits of attending college?student to want to own and use a credit card, and how necessary is it for students to have credit cards?credit card to the student who is enrolled in college.10 I r ~ s cAn article titled "40 Money Management Tips Every College Student Should Know" contained in a book.Know," which was printed in the National Endowment for Financial Education. The writer of the pieceHere, many strategies for keeping the halaocc fund stable were investigated, along with how toTake care of the administration of the funds. 2010 was the year it was first released to the public.There is no getting around the fact that college is very pricey. However, it is feasible to pay for your own thera py.education without jeopardizing your ability to achieve your financial goals in the future. 40 Tips for Effective Financial ManagementYou can go to the Every College Student Should Know resource if you need any help with anything.throughout the year, if you have queries regarding your finances.An Article That Has Been Previously Printed in the Journal of Behavioral Studies in BusinesshStudent budgeting and spending behaviors: a comparative study" is a paper that was written by.Amy Vandenberg of St. Norbert College and Matthew Stollak of St. Norbert College are the authors of this piece.Kevin Steiner from the University of Marquette and Jessica Richards from St. Norbert College.The author of this piece has stated that readers will be free from the conveniences of home. numerous studentsare having their first encounters with being independent of anyone else. One of the difficulties that they face isbudgeting is a matter of face. This becomes an especially difficult situation when a projected budget is involved.item has been updated.This study investigates the ways in which students at a modest liberal arts college in the Midwest meet theproblem with the budgets. How do students organize and allocate their funds for extracurricular activities?than the components that are required? This example demonstrates the behaviors of students and discusses theConsideration is given to the consequences for clinical work.A Research Paper that Was Presented on the

FINANCIAL MANAGEMENT METHODS OFSTUDENTS IN COLLEGE

by Kayla Allen, Southeastern Louisiana University,Southeastern Louisiana University's Victoria Kinchen was just published in GLOBAL JOURNAL.Volume 3 Issue 1 of the Journal of Business Research, 20 09.The author of the article bas claimed that in light of the historically high rates of mortgage default andIt was anticipated that more than one million people in the United States will file for bankruptcy in 2008. It is risk-free to do so.The conclusion is that a large number of American citizens have pushed themselves too far financially. This study is aimed towards.11 1rageexamines the possibility that a large number of Americans are ignorant on the subject. behaviors or routinesfundamental to the successful administration of one's personal finances.The purpose of this study is to determine the factors that led to unethical financial practices andto develop strategies that can aid students at coUegc in improving their financial situationspractices related to management.1.8 Unfilled Research Needs:It has been discovered that a significant portion of the student population that resides in hostels in the city of Pune is facingtheir difficulties with their finances. They either receive a negligible amount as payment for their services or none at all.The amount of money that must be spent is necessary.The researcher has not come across any studies that have been carried out to learn more about the.difficulties confronted by students who reside in hostels throughout the nation. After completing all of that,literature, the researcher discovered that such a survey on hostel residents and students either ontheir financial management practices, banking routines, or any other element of their lives is not investigated. Because of this, the researcher felt compelled to investigate issues of this nature and gain an understanding of them.They are confronted with a wide variety of challenges. because of this, the researcher has decided to look into thechallenges stemming from the poor financial management and banking practices of the host culturestudents in the city of Punctuation. The administration of their financial resources over the course of one month was alsonot investigated; hence, the researcher decided to focus their attention on this particular subject.1.9 Unstated Assumptions:I. Students are knowledgeable about what a bank is and how money operat es.., Their parents give them "a Certain Amount of Money" for day-to-day expenses.the cost incurred. They must rely on another person in order to obtain financial support.3. They are not staying in the house that they own in Puoe, thus they are not living with their parents.4. Every student who makes purchases also sets something aside for the unpredictability of their future need.5. Students who are employed save a greater proportion of their income than students who are not employed.6. The following types of students are included in the research sample:1

. Working—both part time and full time.b. obtained a loan for educational expenses.c. Scholarship for further education was obtained.d. only receiving financial support from their parents.1.10 The aims and objectives of the research1. to investigate the practices of money management, saving, and spending, as well as bankingThe term "habits" will be used to refer to the following characteristics of the students:a) To investigate the characteristics of the pupils with regard to their way of life, the amount ofdependence on the currency. history on the financial front.b) To conduct an in-depth analysis of the various elements that influence the banking behaviors ofstudents at the undergraduate and postgraduate levels in relation to financial mattersthe management.c) To evaluate the banking routines and procedures of both undergraduate and graduate studentsstudents located in the city of Pune.d) To evaluate students' perspectives on financial planning topics such as saves and investments,handling of financial matters.e) To investigate the elements that have an impact on the utilization of banking services or goodswithin the student body2. in order to identify the most effective technique for raising awareness and enhancing moneyThe students' approaches to money management, savings, and banking are examined.3. To make proposals and recommendations for the betterment of the money.management and banking practices practiced by the pupils of the hostel ite.4. The purpose of this research is to investigate the financial issues facing poor, marginalized, and oppressed hostelites.c ollege students.1.11 The Objectives and Their JustificationThe researcher was able to get a comprehensive picture of the student or respondent population thanks to the study.to what sort of history does he have. his family situation, in addition to other personal details, and so on.13 I P;~geFor the purpose of gaining a grasp of their expertise regarding banking routines and information certainquestions as well as the requirements for interactive teclmiques were established and applied here.While conducting research, the surrounding environment in the local sample region provided theinvestigate the facts regarding the many different items and services that are available tocollege students. Are they the same in relation to various regions and streams, or is there a standard for them?the great outdoors.In addition to focusing on spending and saving, the primary goal of this study is money management.putting patterns to save. The primary emphasis would be placed on both their significant and trivial day-to-day costs.the act of operating. Since the subject or respondent will be receiving some monetary compensation from theirmom and dad. He is responsible for managing his particular time duration and spending within those pa rameters.size of. Therefore, it would be helpful to know how and why he handles aU such expenditures. in addition toThe potential for cost cutting measures has also been uncovered.It is also of the utmost importance that banks carry out a variety of important steps on their own.Today, businesses in every sector operate from a customer-service rather than an ownership perspective.a point of view. As a result, there are a variety of measures or plan policies now in place, in addition to additional measures.that need to be carried out were also uncovered and investigated.

Hypothesis Determination Statement:I. Ho: The Hostelite students are aware of and watchful with regard to their financial situationThe adminis tration.There is a lack of awareness and caution on the part of the Hostelite students regarding theirManagement of one's finances.II. Ho: There is a direct connection between the banking practices and thequantity that has been put away for future use.There is no correlation between one's banking practices and the quantity of money that one has.is no longer in danger.14 I "<~ & eltl Ho: Students who are poor, marginalized, and downtrodden are a long way from the mainstream.Managing One's FinancesHl: Students who are poor, marginalized, and downtrodden who are very close to theManaging One's FinancesIV. Ho: Students who are responsible for their own financial management are aware of the importance ofin contrast to students who depend on their parents.Students who are responsible for their own finances often lack awareness in this area.in contrast to students who are dependent on their parents.1.13 Definitions of words for use in working documentsManaging Your Finances:Management of one's finances refers to the process of directing one's financial resources, which may include one'sinvesting involves financial planning, banking, and tax preparation; it is often referred to as a branch of investment.management is another name for the process of budgeting, which is part of money management.Utilization of cash in any way, including spending, saving, investing, managing, or otherwise putting it to useeither that of a single person or that of a group.Depending on the context, one may refer to expenditure as:• The cost is the sum of money or its monetary equivalent that is required to acquire anything.• Expense: the transfer of money from one person to another in order to meet a financial obligation (also known as "covering a cost")• Expenditures for one's own personal use or consumption; one's personal consumption categoryTo saveThe act of putting aside money from one's income rather than spending it immediately is known as saving.Putting money away in a safe place, like a deposit account, is one example of a method that can be used to save.accounL a pension accatmt, an investment fund, or as cash. The most noteworthy and common types of accounts are investment funds and cash.The fact that one must do it on their own accord and out of their own resources is a key aspect of saving.will. You can't just keep crossing your fingers and hope that you'll have some quantity of money left to put away.By the end of the month after deducting all of your expenses, if you make this one of your primary expenses and do

I Have Passedit first. You need to set aside between 10 and 20 percent of your earnings for your retirement and other long-term financial go als.transpired automatically despite one's lack of involvement, resulting in a substantial amount of residualafter a very prolonged time.Education at the Undergraduate LevelThe education received after high school and before graduate study is referred to as under graduate education.education beyond the undergraduate level, which encompasses all of the academic programs and courses completed up tolevel equivalent to that of a bachelor's degree.Education at the postgraduate levelEducation received after completion of one's bachelor's or master's degree is known as postgraduate education.Education beyond the undergraduate level encompasses all of the academic programs available up to the doctoral level.degrees at the bachelor's level and higher are available.The ostellitic:A person who stays in hostels is known as a hostelite, according to Collins. This can be a student or another type of individual.or a person who lives away from his own house or the home of his parents in order to pursue his education or work.a person who stays in a hostel, regardless of the type of hostel, is known as a hostelite.a person who is away from his or her residential or parental home. a person who is staying in a hostel.must be responsible for his or her own

food, clothing, and shelter, as well as for making the necessary arrangeme
nts.In this manner, taking the first step toward becoming self-sufficient is
referred to as "as of a hostehite."Only students that meet the criteria for a
stay in a hostel are included in the current study's participants.above. For
the sake of their education, they have chosen to relocate somewhere other
than their usual residence.about the hostel.Students of the EBC:Students
who fall into the Economically Backward Class category are referred to as
EBC Students. The term "EBC"meaning those whose family income is less
than 8 million rupees belong to this category.to the EBC Category, you will
be eligible for a fee exemption for higher education if you come under this
category.this information or figures are from the most recent notification
and fall within the EBC category.

E.circular issued by the Government of Maharashtra State. the government overall and historically whenrequired is permitted to make periodic
adjustments to this restriction of the maximum allowable income, which is
defined asup top.A custom:A learned behavior or pattern that is followed
with sufficient consistency that it almost seems automatic.a taught behavioral reaction that has become connected with a stimulus but is not within
the control of the individualparticular circumstance, especially one that
occurs frequently. an activity or behavior that is performed repeatedly by
someone.an individual or anyone who repeats a behavior over and again
is considered to have a habit. One routine andAn ongoing pattern of
behavior to perform some task is referred to as a habit.Products Offered
by Banks:Anything that is supplied to a customer in addition to a product
or service is considered to add value to the product or service..new goods
or services to redefine the convenience of banking, combined with experienced knowledgeby making use of technology, you may reassure them that

their welfare is being taken care of and give them peace of mind.safeguard ed and constantly tended to at the same time at the bank; this may either be for the benefit of thevarious accounts, including current accounts, savings accounts, and student accounts, as well as demat accounts.account, Loan, and similar things like that.Services Provided by Banks:Any and all operations in which Mat is engaged in the process of taking and securing the money earnedowned by other well-known individuals and organizations, and, in turn, leasing out miscellaneous items to third partiesActivities or activities that bring in money that can then be turned into a profit for an organization include:offering instant services, including the acceptance of deposits, the issuing of loans or credit, and the crediting ofclearing and in cash, financing or leasing, operations, the stock or securities market, etc. all fall under this category.Student who is dependent:A student who is in need of as well as requires the support, assistance, and help ofsomething or someone that is required in order for it to continue existing or running on a day-to-day basisThose who are unable to carry out their own daily duties are referred to as dependents.17I P~geStudent who is self-sufficient:A student who does not require any kind of support or assistance from anyone else inOne who does not rely on something else in order to continue living or working; independent.Classification of People According to Their Income:According to the regulations set forth by the government, it is categorized and specified in accordance with the family'sconsumption on a per-person basis on a daily basis or their income is what the thresholds and limits are based on.a variety of goods, with Rs. 60 per day being the daily per capita income threshold below which people are considered to be living in poverty.are generally $2 for individuals who are deemed to be poor, and S2-S I 0 ranges from 60-100 to S2-S I 0 rupees.

I 000 in fines for persons who fall into the low-income category. According to these rules and regulations.defrnjtjoo, persons with incomes falling within the middle class are classified as those who, on average,You should aim to make between $10 and $20 every day, depending on how much money your family brings in overall.It's possible to identify or categorize someone's income for a day or for a month as lower, middle, or high.or a person who belongs to the upper class.1.14 The Significance and Significance of the Study• The expansion and development of an economy in any nation is contingent upon the expansion of its agricultural sector.its banking industry; hence, expansion in the banking sector of an economy is directly proportional to expansion in that sector.depends on the amount of money people put away in savings accounts and invest in the stock market.behaviors related to banking that are typical among various segments or sections of the population in thethe community.Why Banks are not rapidly improving their services or technology to the degree that is required by our nation.because of the frequent, time-limited, routine, and ongoing failure of establishment,because of banking practices that are financially irresponsible, risky, and unsound.• People in general have a high level of trust in their ability to conduct business as it currently stands.I did some research and found out that there are alternative ways to get quick money and investments.Therefore, individuals prefer to select for those possibilities rather than conducting business at a physical location.bank Customers should be taught to bank at a young age so that the habit can be ingrained early on.among students in conjunction with educational institutions and educational institutions to encourage saving andbehaviors regarding one's banking.

• One of the most common behaviors seen in college students is a disorganized approach to conserving their money.students. A lot of the time, an amount or some money is put to the side from the point of view of however, they wind up being used for other purposes or in times of emergency instead of being saved.• Another important issue is that students are not financially independent or responsible for their own finances.They have no choice but to rely on their parents for their allowance.Due to the high cost of an A.'s education, some parents begin making preparations for their children's college education from a young age.for their LCIs, while other parents would rather see their children begin working part-time jobs and contributing financially to the household.themselves for further study and advancement in their careers in this way. In this way, they will be able toDevelop your sense of responsibility and self-control.• If students want to save more money, they need to take an honest look at their spending patterns.high standards of living, changing attitudes, and the influence of peers are all things that this generation enjoys.They prefer to put more of their money toward things like food, entertainment, friends, traveling, and shopping.• Another reason for choosing this subject is to investigate people's levels of banking awareness and expertise.products and transactions in addition to the use of it by students.• Some observations regarding students placed in the economically backward category (E.B.C.) would also be appreciated.be carried out that would aid us in identifying the challenges that parents present their children with.colleges, governments, and other social and political viewpoints; an attempt should be made to show howThe banking, spending, and saving habits of EBC countries are distinct from those of non-EBC countries.college students.• Only a small percentage of students are awarded any amount of scholarship money from either educational institution.NGOs and other institutions. A trust is... Govenuncnt (EBC). etc. The scenario with thesestudents is they get an additional handful of amount in which they can managetheir petty expenses.1.15 Scope of the study:The scope of the study is confined to an assessment and analysis of tJ1e moneymanagement and banking habits of the hostelite students from the Pune city. Thepresent study focuses on status of hostelitc students. need of financial education.saving and banking habits among students stay ing on hostels. Later it analyzed in19 I "acedepth banking habits of respondents. Use of ATM. Debit Card. Credit Card.awareness and usc of online and mobile banking were studied in particular.The research study selected will be covering college students who study inundergraduate and postgraduate colleges in Punc. This limits the scope of study toother diverse and other courses colleges in the city.The researcher has undertaken this study to a ll hostels in city of punc. There arestudents coming from different areas of Pune Districts . Other Cities or districts andvillages from Maharashtra. ln today's modernised era we can also see studentscoming from across lndia and even abroad i.e. western or foreign countries too.Hence all types of students are taken for study and aspect as to banking habit andmoney management is studied in detai l.1.16 Limitations of the study:I. The study is related to students in Pune city only.1 The research is undertaken for undergraduate and post graduate students. Otherstudents doing professional studies are not taken for stud y.3. Only hostelite students are taken for study. It limits the scope to local residentcollege students.4. The current study is related only for 3 years that is 2015- 16, 20 16-1 7 & 2017-18.5. Study is undertaken for only one aspect that is Banking Habits . other aspects orareas are not sntdied.

Classes of respondents to be contacted:I) Age group is between 18-21.2) All Classes such as High, Medium and Low income class or students .3) Students perusing their Undergraduate and Postgraduate courses.4) Students from any stream such as Arts. Science. Commerce. Engg. Pha nnaey.Medical, Law, Computers and So on.20 1 r :~ g e5) Local I State I Inter & lntra State I National and Foreign students would alsoconsist of the sample.6) Public and private sector Banks in Pune City.7) 10-15% of all types ofhostel in Pune city.1.18 Universe & sample size:Universe/ Population: Students studying in colleges and those s1aying on hostels inthe city of Pune.Ta ble No: 1.1Table displaying the differ ent types of dormitories and their numbers in PuneSr. No. Types of Hostel Qua ntity I No. of Hostels1 Boys/Gents 482 Girls/Ladies 393 Poor/Econo- my Class 244 Caste Based Hostel 185 Private Hostel 95 Private Hostel6 In-Area Expertise 2306 Mixed-Gender Hostel 78 Welfare and Social Ser- vices 329 Educational Institutions and Their Premises 180NRI Hostel No. 10 Room 5411 Individuals with Severe Disabilities 3412 Getting On Board 2213 Employees and 35 Non-Employees610 in totalResearcher of Surveillance Systems as the Source21 I'm going to Pat'eAn optimal sample size for this research was determined to be 800 students, and a survey was conducted with those students.In addition, the technique of simple random sampling was implemented whenever it was possible to guarantee thedegree of precision or exactness.About 10–15% of each hostel category type has been sampled for this study. The list of hostels can be found here.The information regarding the hostels that were used for the study can be found appended to the thesis in the annexure.The 1.2 tableA table illustrating the various categories of respondents who participated in the researchQuantity of Seniors and ClassesWho are working one hundred2

Obtained a student loan for a total of 1003 students were awarded scholarships totaling 1004 of them received money from their parents totaling 500800 in totalThe Researcher Carried Out a Survey.1.19 A Defense of the Sampling Method and the Sampling ProcedureThe method of sampling consisted of a combination of random sampling and sampling based on judgment.In addition, a method known as stratified random sampling was utilized so that srudents may be chosen.The state of Maharashtra is the second largest in terms of both its population and its total geographical area.Mumbai is the capital of India and has a population of 11.24 crore people (Census 20l).

Mumbai is the state capital of Maharashtra and the financial hub of India. It is also the location of the headquarters of many major Indian companies.It is the most populated city in India and is home to numerous large corporations and financial organizations.I am on page 22The primary stock exchange in India. the stock exchange as well as the commodity exchange. This is one of them.the top 10 commercial hubs throughout the world in terms of the volume of international money moving through the m.Pune is a city located close to Mumbai, the state capital of Maharashtra, and contributes 6. 16% of India's GDP.not only provides opportunities for company but also helps thousands of people find employment in the proc ess.would entice people to move there from different parts of India.Because of this, young people currently enrolled in higher education in the city of Pune have been chosen to participate in the study.Pune, widely known as the "Oxford of the Castes," is home to a large number of students who are considered to represent the young of India.aspirants who are looking forward to furthering their studies or exploring their options come topune for ruslher higher education.

CHAPTER TWO

Bank

A financial entity that accepts deposits from the general public and establishes a demand deposit while simultaneously providing loans is referred to be a bank. [1] Lending activities can either be directly undertaken by the bank or indirectly through the capital markets.In light of the fact that banks play a crucial part in the financial stability and economic growth of a nation, the majority of jurisdictions subject banks to a significant amount of regulation. The majority of nations have formalized what is known as a fractional-reserve banking system, which mandates that financial institutions keep liquid assets that are only equivalent to a percentage of their total current liabilities. In addition to the various laws that are meant to assure liquidity, banks are normally subject to minimum capital requirements that are based on an international set of capital standards known as the Basel Accords.Banking in its modern sense developed in the fourteenth century in the rich cities of Renaissance Italy, but in many ways it functioned as a continuation of ideas and conceptions of credit and lending that had their roots in the ancient world. Banking in its modern sense evolved in the fourteenth century in the prosperous cities of Renaissance Italy. Throughout the course of the history of banking, a number of banking families, most notably the Medicis, the Fuggers, the Welsers, the Berenbergs, and the Rothschilds, have been instrumental for a significant amount of time and have played a pivotal role. The Banca Monte dei Paschi di Siena, which was established in 1472, is now the world's oldest retail bank. The Berenberg Bank, which was established in 1590, is currently the world's oldest merchant bank. The past:[icon]The history of the period following the 19th century should be added to this section. You can be of assistance by contributing to it. (8th of August, 2020)The history of banking can be found in the main article.During the process of cleaning out the temple, the money-changers depicted in this artwork from the 15th century are seated on a banca.It is believed that banking as an ancient activity (or quasi-banking) began anywhere between the later half of the fourth millennium BCE and the third millennia BCE.

Middle Ages

The origins of the modern era of banking may be traced back to the prosperous towns of central and northern Italy, such as Florence, Lucca, Siena, Venice, and Genoa. This was during the middle ages and the early Renaissance. Giovanni di Bicci de' Medici established one of the most famous Italian banks, the Medici Bank, in 1397.[8] The Republic of Genoa founded the earliest-known state deposit bank, Banco di San Giorgio (Bank of St. George), in 1407 at Genoa, Italy. [9] The Bardi and Peruzzi families dominated banking in 14th-century Florence, establishing branches in many other parts of Europe.Before the modern eraLady Jane Lindsay's painting depicting the Bank of England Charter being sealed in 1694 was completed in 1905.The use of banknotes and the development of fractional reserve banking both took place in the 17th and 18th centuries. The gold that merchants owned began to be stored by the goldsmiths of London, who owned private vaults and demanded a fee for the service. Goldsmiths in London possessed these vaults. In exchange for each deposit of precious metal, the goldsmiths issued receipts that certified the quantity and purity of the metal they held as bailee; these receipts could not be assigned, and only the original depositor could recover the stored goods. The goldsmiths acted as bailees for the precious metals.Promissory notes, which eventually evolved into banknotes, were produced in exchange for money placed with goldsmiths as a form of a loan to the goldsmith. Gradu-ally, the goldsmiths started lending money out on behalf of the depositor. Thus, by the 19th century, we find that in ordinary cases of deposits of money with banking corporations or bankers, the transaction amounts to a mere loan or mutuum, and the bank is to restore, not the same money, but an equivalent sum, whenever it is demanded[10]. Furthermore, mon-ey that is paid into a bank ceases altogether to be the money of the principal (see Parker v. Marchant, 1 Phillips 360); it is then the money of the banker, who is bound to return The goldsmith offered interest payments on customer deposits. This was an early type of fractional reserve banking due to the fact that the promissory notes had to be paid back immediately, whereas the advances (loans) made to the goldsmith's customers could be paid back over a longer period of time. The promissory notes eventually developed into an assignable instrument that could circulate as a safe and convenient form of money[12] backed by the goldsmith's promise to pay, allowing goldsmiths to advance loans with little risk of default. [14] [need quotation to verify] As a result, the goldsmiths of London became the forerunners of banking by creating new money based on credit.During the 1910s, this was the interior of the Helsinki Branch of the Vyborg-Bank [fi].In 1695, the Bank of England was the first financial institution to issue banknotes on a permanent basis.

In 1728, the Royal Bank of Scotland established the first overdraft facility. [16] At the beginning of the 19th century, Lubbock's Bank established a bankers' clearing house in London to make it possible for multiple financial institutions to clear transactions simultaneously. The Rothschild family was a pioneer in the field of international banking on a massive scale. In 1875, they provided the British government with the funding necessary to purchase shares in the Suez canal. [need quotation to verify]The origins of a wordMiddle English bank came from the Middle French term banque, which was derived from the Old Italian word banco, which meant "table," and from the Old High German banc, bank, which meant "bench, counter." During the Renaissance, Florentine bankers would make their transactions on tables that were covered in green tablecloths. [20][21] Benches were employed as makeshift desks or exchange counters during this time period by the Florentine bankers.The meaning ofThe concept of a bank can be understood differently in different nations. For further information, please refer to the websites pertaining to the appropriate countries.Banker is described as a person who carries on the business of banking by conducting current accounts for their clients, cashing cheques drawn on them, and also collecting cheques for their customers under the common law of England. [22] This definition of banker comes from the English common law.The Coro branch of the Venezuelan Central

Bank.Pokhara, located in western Nepal, is home to a Nepal Bank branch.There is a Bills of Exchange Act in most common law jurisdictions that codifies the law in relation to negotiable instruments, such as checks. This Act contains a statutory definition of the term banker, which states that "banker includes a body of persons, whether incorporated or not, who carry on the business of banking" (Section 2, Interpretation). Checks are an example of a negotiable instrument. Although this definition appears to be circular, in practice, it serves a practical purpose. Namely, it assures that the legal basis for bank transactions such as cheques does not depend on the organizational structure or regulatory environment of the bank. In many nations governed by common law, the banking industry is not defined by statute but rather by common law, as the definition presented above explains. There are statutory definitions of the banking business or banking business in different jurisdictions that follow the English common law tradition. When looking at these definitions, it is essential to keep in mind that they are defining the banking industry for the purposes of the legislation, and not necessarily in a generic sense.

This is important to keep in mind because it is vital to keep in mind that they are defining the banking industry. In particular, the majority of the definitions come from pieces of law whose primary focus is on the regulation and supervision of financial institutions like banks, as opposed to the regulation of the banking industry itself. On the other hand, in many instances, the legislative definition substantially resembles the one provided by common law. Some examples of statutory definitions include the following:"banking business" is defined as the business of receiving money on current or deposit account, paying and collecting cheques drawn by or paid in by customers, the making of advances to customers, and includes such other business as the Authority may prescribe for the purposes of this Act; (Banking Act (Singapore), Section 2, Interpretation). This definition can be found in the Banking Act (Singapore), Section 2.The term "banking business" refers to the operations of any or both of the following types of businesses:accepting money from members of the general public on a current account, deposit account, savings account, or other account of a similar nature that is repayable on demand or within less than [three mo nths].... alternatively, with a term of call or notice that is shorter than that period;clients' checks can be cashed or collected if they have been written or deposited by the consumer. [23]Since the introduction of technologies such as EFTPOS (Electronic Funds Transfer at Point of Sale), direct credit, direct debit, and internet banking, the cheque's status as the primary mode of payment in the majority of banking systems has been demoted.

As a result of this, legal theorists have proposed that the term of "cheque-based" should be widened to encompass financial organizations that operate current accounts for clients and enable consumers to pay and be paid by third parties, even if these institutions do not pay and collect cheques. [24]The usual course of eventsMassive entrance leading to the vault of an antique bank.The provision of checking and current accounts to customers, the payment of cheques drawn by customers on the bank, and the collection of cheques placed to customers' current accounts are all examples of how banks fulfill their role as payment agents. The Automated Clearing House (ACH), wire transfers, telegraphic transfers, electronic funds transfer point-of-sale (EFTPOS), and automated teller machines (ATMs) are some of the other payment methods that customers of banks can utilize to make payments.The most common ways for financial institu- tions to obtain funds for lending are through the acceptance of cash put on current accounts, the acceptance of term deposits, and the issuance of debt securities such as banknotes and bonds. Banks lend money to consumers in a variety of ways, including by providing advances to customers on their current accounts, making installment loans, investing in marketable debt securities, and providing other types of loans and advances.Banks offer a variety of payment services, and having a bank account is seen as absolutely necessary by the vast majority of businesses and individuals. It is not common practice to view non-banking institutions that offer payment services, such as remittance businesses, as a suitable alternative to having a checking account with a bank.When they give out loans, banks create brand new units of currency. In today's modern banking systems, regulators are responsible for establishing a minimum level of reserve funds that banks are required to keep against the deposit liabilities caused by the funding of these loans. The goal of this requirement is to ensure that banks are able to fulfill the requirements for payment of deposits when they become due. These reserves can be obtained in a number of different ways, including the taking of additional deposits, the selling of other assets, or borrowing money from other banks, including the central bank. [25]Various kinds of activitiesPersonal banking, corporate banking, investment banking, private banking, transaction banking, insurance, consumer financing, trade finance, and other related activities are all examples of banking services that are provided by banks.Routes and PassagesAn American bank located in the state of Maryland.The following are some of the many different access points that banks provide to their banking and other services:Personal, face-to-face banking at a branch or retail locationThe use of automated teller machines for banking can take place either adjacent to or away from the bank.The vast majority of financial institutions welcome check deposits sent through the mail and rely on mail as their primary method of customer communication.

Utilizing the Internet to conduct financial transactions of a wide variety through online banking.Mobile banking is the practice of conducting banking transactions via a mobile device, such as a smartphone.Custo mers who use telephone banking are able to complete transactions over the phone with the assistance of an automated attendant or, if they so want, with a telephone operator.Through the use of a remote video and voice link, customers can complete banking transactions or consult with banking professionals through the use of video banking. It is possible to do video banking either using specially designed banking transaction machines (which function in a manner analogous to that of an automated teller machine) or through a bank branch that is equipped with video con- ferencing technology.Relationship manager, typically employed by private banking or business banking, who makes personal visits to clients' places of business or residencesDirect Selling Agents are independent contractors who work for the bank under a contract and whose primary responsibility it is to grow the bank's customer base.Modes of doing businessA bank's revenue can be increased through a variety of channels, such as through the collection of interest, the charging of transaction fees, and the provision of financial advisory services. Charging interest on the capital that it lends out to clients has traditionally been the most significant technique. [26] The bank makes a profit from the difference between the level of interest it pays for deposits and other sources of funds, and the level of interest it charges in its lending activities.The difference between the interest rate on the loan and the cost of the money is referred to as the spread between the two. Throughout history, the profitability of lending activities has historically followed cyclical patterns and been highly dependent on the requirements and capabilities of loan customers in addition to the stage of the economic cycle. Because fees and financial advice represent a more reliable revenue stream, banks have shifted their focus to concentrate more of their efforts on these revenue lines in order to smooth out their overall financial performance.

Over the course of the past two decades, American banks have used a wide variety of strategies in an effort to preserve their profitability while also adapting to the ever-shifting conditions of the market.To begin, this includes the Gramm–Leach–Bliley Act, which makes it possible once more for financial institutions to combine forces with investment and insurance firms. Traditional banks are able to meet the growing demand from customers for "one-stop shopping" by combining their banking, investing, and insurance activities. This allows for the cross-selling of products, which the banks believe will also boost their profitability.Second, they have extended the use of risk-based pricing from business lending to consumer lending. This means that they will charge higher interest rates to clients who are viewed as having a larger credit risk and therefore an increased probability of defaulting on loans. Previously, this pricing strategy was only used for business lending. This serves to mitigate the losses that are incurred from poor loans, decreases the price of loans for those who have superior credit records, and extends credit products to high risk clients who would otherwise be denied credit.Thirdly, they have made it a priority to broaden the range of payment processing options that are open to commercial customers as well as the general public. Cards such as debit cards, prepaid cards, smart cards, and credit cards are included in these products. They make it simpler for consumers to carry out transactions in a convenient manner and to smooth out their consumption over time (in some nations with underdeveloped financial systems, it is nevertheless normal practice to deal exclusively in cash, including lugging suitcases full of cash to purchase a home).On the other hand, despite the fact that consumers have easier access to credit, there is a greater chance that they will fail to properly manage their financial resources and end up with an excessive amount of debt. Banks generate revenue from card products through the collection of interest and other fees from cardholders, as well as through the collection of transaction fees from retailers who accept the bank's credit cards and debit cards as forms of payment.This makes it easier to turn a profit and contributes to the overall growth and development of the economy.

Recently, as banks have been put under pressure by fintechs, new and additional business models have been suggested. Some of these models include freemium, monetisation of data, white-labeling of banking and payment applications, or the cross-selling of complementary items. [29] In addition to these models, cross-selling complementary products has also been recommended.Items for saleA retail banking institution that was formerly a building society and is located in Leeds, West Yorkshire.A portion of the inside of a National Westminster Bank location in Liverpool located on Castle StreetThe retail sector.card for use at ATMsCards de crédit-Card de débitAccount for savingsAccount that accepts regular deposit-sAccounts for fixed depositsAccounts on the money marketA certificate of deposit, sometimes known as a CD.Individual Retirement Account (IRA), also abbreviated as IRAMortgage loan.Investment companyLoans against personal property (also known as secured and unsecured personal loans)Payroll deductionsThe most recent accountsChecks and checkbooksThe abbreviation for "automated teller machine" (ATM)The National Electronic Fund Transfer, also abbreviated as NEFT,The Real-Time Gross Settlement, or RTGS, abbreviates.Banking for businesses (sometimes known as commercial or investment banking)Loan to a business-Methods of raising capital (equity, debt, and hybrids)Credit on a rotating basisForeign exchange (FX), interest rates, commodities, and derivatives all fall within the purview of risk management.Loan on a term basisServices related to the management of cash, such as safe deposit boxes, remote deposit capture, and merchant processing.Services related to creditServices Relating to SecuritiesInvesting and taking risksStructures unique to banking institutionsRisk in the market

FRTB

The internal models approach, often known as the IMA,standardized method for assessing market riskThe danger of creditIRB stands for "internal ratings-based approach."The Foundation Institutional Review Board, or F-IRB,A-IRB stands for advanced IRB.A standardized method for assessing credit riskCredit exposure to a counterpartyThe currently employed exposure method, or CEMSM stands for "standardized meth od."Standardized approach to (counterparty credit risk), abbreviated as SA-CCRThe risk of operationsAMA stands for advanced measurement approach.Approach Primarily Based on IndicatorsApproach standardization (level of operational risk)SMA stands for the standardized measurement approach.vteAdditional resources: management of financial risk bankingSee also: Risk management in the field of finance and risk management in the field of investment banking.In order for banks to carry out their business, they are exposed to a multitude of risks. The efficiency with which these risks are handled and comprehended is a significant factor in determining a bank's profitability as well as the minimum amount of capital it is necessary to keep on hand. The three main components that make up a bank's capital are equity, retained earnings, and subordinated debt.The following are some of the most significant dangers that banks face:Credit risk is defined as the potential for financial loss resulting from a borrower's failure to make payments as agreed upon [30].Liquidity risk is the possibility that a particular security or asset will not be able to be traded in the market quickly enough to avoid a loss (or make the necessary profit) in a timely manner.Market risk is defined as the possibility that the value of a portfolio, whether it be an investment portfolio or a trading portfolio, may go down as a result of a change in the value of market risk variables.Risk that results from the day-to-day activities of running a firm is referred to as operational risk.A sort of risk that is associated with the reliability of the organization is known as reputational risk.Risks associated with the overall economy in which the bank operates are referred to as macroeconomic risk.

A bank or other depository institution is required to manage its balance sheet in accordance with the regulations that make up the capital requirement. These regulations provide a framework for doing so. In order to facilitate the application of risk weighting, the classification of assets and capital has been subjected to stringent standardization.Following the global financial crisis that occurred between 2007 and 2008, regulatory agencies ordered banks to issue contingent convertible bonds, also known as CoCos. When the capital of the issuing bank falls below a specific level, these hybrid capital instruments start to absorb losses in accordance with the conditions of their contracts. After that, the amount of debt is decreased, and the capitalization of the banks is increased. CoCos have the potential to satisfy regulatory capital requirements because of their ability to absorb losses[32][33].Banks in the context of the economy The primary headquarters of SEB in Tallinn, Estonia See also: the monetary and economic system The workings of the economy The following are examples of the economic roles that banks play:The creation of money, in the form of banknotes and current accounts, which may be paid for with a check or paid in full at the request of the consumer. Because these claims on banks are negotiable and may be repaid on demand, they can be used as a form of money because their value remains constant. They can be effectively transferred either through the act of simple delivery, as is the case with banknotes, or by the writing of a check that the payee can either deposit or cash.Payment instruments are netted and settled when banks participate in interbank clearing and settlement systems to collect, present, be presented with, and pay payment instruments. During this process, banks function as both collection and paying agents for their customers. Because of this, banks are able to make more efficient use of the reserves they keep for the settlement of payments because incoming and outgoing payments cancel each other out. Additionally, it makes it possible to offset payment flows between geographical locations, which in turn lowers the cost of settlement between such areas.Credit quality is improved when banks lend money to regular commercial and personal borrowers (borrowers with ordinary credit quality), yet these borrowers have high credit quality themselves.

The improvement is due to the bank's increased level of asset and capital diversification, which offers a buffer that allows the bank to absorb losses without defaulting on its obligations. However, banknotes and deposits are not normally secured by anything. If the bank runs into financial trouble and has to pledge assets as security in order to acquire the capital it needs to continue to operate, this places the holders of the banknotes and depositors in a position that is economically below that of the bank. Mismatch in assets and liabilities, also known as maturity transformation, occurs when financial institutions borrow more in the form of demand and short-term debt but lend more in the form of long-term loans. To put it another way, they borrow money quickly and lend it out slowly. This can be accomplished by aggregating issues (such as accepting deposits and issuing banknotes) and redemptions (such as withdrawals and redemption of banknotes), maintaining cash reserves, investing in marketable securities that can be readily converted to cash if necessary, and raising replacement funding as needed from various sources (such as wholesale cash markets and securities markets). Banks have a higher credit quality than the majority of other borrowers, so they are better able to accomplish this goal.Whenever a bank in a system that uses fractional reserves extends credit to a customer, a new quantity of money is produced. On the other hand, money is eliminated whenever the main balance of an existing loan is paid back in full. This process is known as the creation and destruction of money.Financial crisisOTP Bank in Prev (Slovakia), located in Prev.Banks are susceptible to many different types of risk, some of which have been known to cause occasional systemic crises. [34] These risks include liquidity risk (which occurs when many depositors may request withdrawals in excess of available funds), credit risk (the possibility that those who owe money to the bank will not repay it), and interest rate risk (the possibility that the bank will become unprofitable, if rising interest rates force it to pay relatively more on its deposits than it receives on its loans).Throughout the course of history, numerous instances of banking crises have arisen as a result of the emergence of one or more dangers for the banking industry as a whole. Notable instances include the bank robbery that took place during the Great Depression and the economic crisis that hit the United States in 2008. The Savings and Loan crisis of the 1980s and early 1990s, the banking crisis that Japan experienced in the 1990s, and the subprime mortgage crisis that occurred in the 2000s are all examples of financial crises.The most recent of these crises was the global financial crisis of 2023.

In March 2023, liquidity shortages and bank insolvencies led to the fall of three banks in the United States. Within two weeks, six of the world's top institutions failed or were shut down by regulators.The magnitude of the international banking industryDuring the 2008–2009 fiscal year, the assets of the 1,000 largest banks in the world increased by 6.8% to a record $96.4 trillion, but profits decreased by 85% to 115 billion dollars. The majority of the growth in assets, notwithstanding the challenging market conditions, may be attributed to recapitalization. In 2008–2009, EU banks owned the highest share of the total, 56%, which was a decrease from their previous year's share of 61%. During the course of the year, the share held by Asian banks climbed from 12% to 14%, while the share held by US banks increased from 11% to 13%. The overall amount of fee revenue generated by global investment in banking was $66.3 billion in 2009, representing a 12% increase compared to the previous year's total [35].This is an indication of the geography and regulatory structure of the United States, which results in a large number of small to medium-sized institutions in its banking system. The United States has the most banks in the world in terms of institutions (5,330 as of 2015) and possibly branches

(81,607 as of 2015). As of the month of November in 2009, the main four banks in China had a combined total of almost 67,000 branches (ICBC:18000+, BOC:12000+, CCB:13000+, and ABC:24000+), and there were an additional 140 smaller banks with an unknown number of branches. There were 129 banks and 12,000 branches spread out across Japan. In 2004, Germany, France, and Italy each had more than 30,000 branches, which was more than quadruple the number of branches that were present in the United Kingdom, which only had 15,000 branches.

Consolidation through mergers and purchasesBanks were involved in about 28,798 mergers or acquisitions between the years 1985 and 2018, acting either as the buyer or the target company in these transactions. The total amount that can be estimated to have been gained from these transactions is approximately 5,169 billion dollars. USD.[37] In terms of value, there have been two significant waves (1999 and 2007), and the highest point of each wave was approximately 460 billion USD. USD thereafter had a sharp decrease (a decrease of 82% between 2007 and 2 018).The following is a list of the most significant financial transactions in history, ranked by value, in which at least one bank was involved:Date of the announcement Name of the acquirer Name of the industry the acquirer works in Target name Target industry Target nation Value of the deal in millions of dollars25 April 2007 RFS Holdings BV Other financials Netherlands 98,189.19 ABN-AMRO Holding N.V. Banks Netherlands1998-04-06 Travelers Group Inc Insurance United States Citicorp Banks United States 72,558.18 dollars29 September 2014 UBS AG Banks Switzerland 65,891.51 UBS AG [clarification needed] Banks Switzerland1998-04-13 Banks United States BankAmerica Corp Banks United States 61,633.40 NationsBank Corp Banks United States Charlotte,

North Carolina Banks United States14 January 2004 Banks United States JPMorgan Chase & Co. Banks United States Bank One Corp., Chicago, Illinois Banks United States 58,663.15Bank of America Corporation, Banks in the United States FleetBoston Financial Corporation, Banks in the State of Massachusetts Banks in the United States 49,260.6314 September 2008 Bank of America Corp., United States Banks Merrill Lynch & Co., Inc., United States Brokerage 48,766.151999-10-13: Sumitomo Bank Ltd., Sakura Bank Ltd., Banks of Japan 45,494.36HM Treasury, a national agency of the United Kingdom, Royal Bank of Scotland Group, and United Kingdom banks, on February 26th, 2009, 41,878.65Banks Japan UFJ Holdings Inc. Mitsubishi Tokyo Financial Group Banks Japan 41,431.03 on February 18, 2005Regulatory ExplicitnessArticle principal: Regulation of Financial InstitutionsAdditionally, refer to Basel II.At the present time, commercial banks are required to hold a specialized banking license in order to conduct business in the majority of legal jurisdictions worldwide.A Framework Based on BaselStandards of international regulation applicable to banks Basel Accords Basel I Basel II Basel

III LCRNSFRFRTB Basel

Basel Committee on Banking Supervision Basel I Basel II Basel III Basel 3.1The SituationRisk and risk management Banking and financial regulations Monetary policy and the central bank Risk and risk managementFirst and foremost, regulatory capitalCapital requirement Capital ratioLeverage ratioTier 1Tier 2Credit risk SA-CRIRB F-IRBA-IRBEAD SA-CCRIMMCCFMarket risk StandardizedIMACVA volOperational risk BasicStandardizedAMA Capital requirement Capital ratioLeverage ratioTier 1Tier 2Credit risk SA-CRIRB F-IRBA-IRBEAD SA-CCRIMMCCFSupervisory assessment constitutes Pillar 2Economic capitalRisk associated with liquidityLegal riskDisclosure to the market is the third pillar.Public disclosurePortal for Business and Economic DiscussionsvteThe acceptance of deposits, even if they are not repayable to the customer's request, is typically considered part of the banking industry when it comes to regulatory purposes. On the other hand, money lending on its own is typically excluded from the definition of banking.In contrast to the majority of other sectors that require government oversight, financial markets generally include a regulator that is also a player in the market. This regulator might be a central bank that is either publicly or privately administered. In most cases, the business of issuing banknotes is also a monopoly that is held by central banks. On the other hand, this is not the case in a number of countries. In the United Kingdom, for instance, the Financial Services Authority is in charge of issuing banking licenses. Furthermore, certain commercial banks, such as the Bank of Scotland, also print their own banknotes in addition to those printed by the Bank of England, which is the central bank of the United Kingdom's goverment.Basel serves as the location of the Bank for International Settlements's global headquarters.A contractual examination of the relationship between the bank (described above) and the customer (defined as any entity for which the bank agrees to conduct an account) is the foundation of banking law. The customer is any entity for which the bank agrees to conduct an account.The following rights and responsibilities are included into this partnership by the legal system:When a customer's bank account is in a credit position, the bank owes the balance to the customer; when the account is in an overdrawn position, the customer owes the balance to the bank. The balance of a customer's bank account represents the financial situation between the customer and the bank.The bank guarantees that it will pay the customer's checks up to the amount that is now available in the customer's account, in addition to any overdraft limit that has been previously agreed upon.

Without a directive from the customer, such as a check written out in the customer's name, the bank is not permitted to withdraw money from the customer's account.The customer authorizes the bank to act as their agent in the collection of cheques that have been deposited into their account, and the bank undertakes to swiftly collect these cheques and credit the proceeds to the client's account.In addition, the financial institution has the legal authority to combine the customer's accounts because each account is merely an individual facet of the overall credit relationship.If the client owes money to the bank, the bank has the right to keep any checks that are placed into the customer's account as collateral until the obligation is paid off.Unless the customer gives their permission, there is a public responsibility to disclose, the bank's interests need it, or the law requires it, the bank is not allowed to disclose the specifics of the transactions that have taken place through the customer's account.Due to the fact that checks are often held up for several days in the normal course of business, the bank is not permitted to shut a customer's account without providing them with adequate notice.These implicit contractual provisions are open to modification, provided that the consumer and the bank come to an unambiguous agreement to do so. The statutes and regulations that are currently in effect within a given jurisdiction may also amend the terms that have been outlined above or establish new rights, obligations, or limitations that are pertinent to the relationship between the bank and the customer.

It's possible for certain kinds of financial institutions, such credit unions and building societies, to be exempt from the bank license requirements entirely or in part. As a result, these institutions are governed by a different set of regulations. The requirements necessary to obtain a license to operate a bank might vary from jurisdiction to jurisdiction, but often include the following: Required amount of capital Required minimum amount of capital Compliance with "Fit and Proper" standards is required of the bank's controllers, owners, directors, and senior executives. Acceptance of the bank's business plan on the grounds that it demonstrates an appropriate level of caution and plausibility. Several distinct kinds of banking This advertisement for Northern National Bank appeared in a book published in 1921 that highlighted the various opportunities that were available in Toledo, Ohio.

- *The following categories can be used to classify banks' activities:*

- *retail banking, which involves interacting directly with customers (such as private individuals or small enterprises);*

- *business banking, or the provision of services to businesses operating in the middle market;*

- *financial services geared toward corporations and other major businesses;*

- *private banking, which consists of offering services in the field of wealth management to high-net-worth individuals and families*

- *investment banking is banking that deals with transactions that take place on various financial markets.*

- *The vast majority of financial institutions are run as profitable private businesses.*

- *On the other hand, some of them are owned by the government, and others are charitable organizations.*

- *Various kinds of banks*

- *Salt Lake City branch of the National Bank of the Republic, 1908*

- *Nuuk Branch of the Bank of Greenland*

- *Mariehamn, land, is home to a branch of the Nordea bank.*

- *ATM located in Al-Rjhi Bank*

- *1911: Opening of the National Copper Bank in Salt Lake City*

A location of the Union Bank in the city of Visakhapatnam

Commercial banks are another name for regular banks; the phrase "commercial bank" is used to differentiate them from investment banks. Following the calamity of the Great Depression, the U.S. Congress mandated that financial institutions only engage in banking-related operations, whereas investment banks might only participate in activities related to the capital markets. Some people use the phrase "commercial bank" to refer to a bank or a subsidiary of a bank that primarily deals with deposits and loans from companies or major businesses. This is because the two no longer need to be under separate ownership, hence the requirement for this distinction has been eliminated. Community banks are financial institutions that are operated on a local level and give its staff the authority to make choices on a local level to better serve their clients and business partners. Community development banks are regulated banks that offer financial services and loans to markets or populations that are not adequately served by traditional banking institutions. Land development banks, sometimes known as LDBs for short, are specialized banks that provide long-term loans to real estate developers. The LDB has a long and illustrious history. In 1920, Jhang, located in Punjab, became the site of the first LDB. The primary purpose of land development banks (LDBs) is to encourage the expansion of agricultural practices and land use, as well as to boost overall agricultural output. Long-term financing is made immediately available to members of the LDBs through the organization's branches Credit unions and co-operative banks are examples of depositor-owned, not-for-profit cooperatives that frequently provide rates that are more favorable than those provided by for-profit banks. In most cases, membership is limited to people who fall into one of the following categories: people who work for a specific company, people who live in a particular region, people who are members of a particular labor union or religious organization, and members of their immediate relatives.

Savings banks that are affiliated with national postal systems are referred to as postal savings banks.

Private banks are financial institutions that specialize in the management of high-net-worth individuals' assets. Historically, the minimum amount needed to create an account was one million United States dollars (US$); however, in recent years, several private banks have reduced the entry obstacles for private investors to three hundred fifty thousand dollars (US$) Offshore banks are defined as banks that are located in countries or territories that have lax taxation and regulatory standards. A significant number of offshore banks are, in essence, private banks. Banks of saves: the origins of savings banks in Europe can be traced back to the 19th century, and in some cases even farther, to the 18th century. Their first goal was to make savings products readily available to people of all social classes and income levels in the society. In some nations, savings banks were established as a result of public initiative, while in others, socially engaged people established foundations in order to put the required infrastructure into place. At this point in time, European savings banks have maintained their concentration on retail banking, which includes the provision of payment services, savings products, credit, and insurance to people as well as to small and medium-sized businesses. In addition to this retail-centric approach, they differentiate themselves from commercial banks in a number of other ways, including the widely decentralized distribution network they utilize to provide local and regional outreach, as well as the socially responsible approach they take to both business and society. Retail banking is carried out by a variety of organisations including building societies and Landesbanks. Ethical banks are financial institutions that place a premium on maintaining complete operational transparency and limit their investment activities to those that they believe to be of a socially responsible nature. A banking organization that does not have any physical bank branches is known as a direct bank or an internet-only bank. In most cases, transactions are completed through the use of automated teller machines (ATMs), electronic transfers, and direct deposits made through an internet interface.

There are various types of investment banks.

Investment banks "underwrite" (ensure the sale of) stock and bond issues, provide investment management services, and advise firms on capital market activities such as mergers and acquisitions. Additionally, investment banks trade for their own accounts, make markets, and provide securities services to institutional clients. Historically speaking, banks that participated in trade finance were known as merchant banks. The current term, on the other hand, refers to financial institutions that make capital available to businesses not in the form of loans but rather as shares. They do not typically invest in new businesses, in contrast to venture capitalists.

Combined banking systems

A branch of the Brazilian bank Banco do Brasil may be found in the city of Sao Paulo. Banco do Brasil is the largest financial organization in both Brazil and Latin America. Many of these pursuits are carried out by universal banks, which are also sometimes referred to as financial services businesses. Bancassurance is a portmanteau word that combines the words "banque or bank" and "assurance," suggesting that both banking and insurance are offered by the same corporate organization. These large banks are very varied groupings that, among other things, also distribute insurance. This is where the phrase "bancassurance" comes from.

Other kinds of banking institutions

Central banks are typically owned by the government and are tasked with quasi-regulatory obligations. These responsibilities can include monitoring commercial banks or determining the interest rate on cash deposits. In general, they are responsible for the provision of liquidity to the banking system and serve as the lender of last resort in the event of an emergency. The principles of Islamic law are followed by Islamic financial institutions. This type of banking is structured around a number of well-established principles that are derived from Islamic law. Interest is a concept that is prohibited in Islam, hence any and all banking activity must steer clear of it. Instead, the bank makes money off of the financing options that it

provides for its customers in the form of both a profit (markup) and fees
Obstacles confronting the financial services sector

Icon of a globe.

It's possible that the examples and points of view shown in this section don't reflect the topic in its entirety everywhere in the world. You are free to make changes to this section, discuss the matter on the page where it is discussed, or establish a new section, as the case may be. (This message was initially published in September 2009; find out how and why it was removed) There are no citations for any sources in this section. Please contribute to the improvement of this section by adding citations to sources that can be trusted. Content that lacks appropriate citations may be contested and removed. (September 2008) (Find out when this message should be removed, as well as how to do it Brooklyn, New York City location of Citibank, in the building formerly occupied by the People's Trust Company. The banking business in the United States is one of the most extensively regulated and guarded in the world[40], with various regulators who specialize in different areas and are focused on those areas. The Federal Deposit Insurance Corporation (FDIC) acts as a regulator for all banks that accept deposits that are guaranteed by the FDIC. The Office of the Comptroller of the Currency (OCC) is the major federal regulator for national banks, but the Federal Reserve is the primary federal regulator for Fed-member state banks when it comes to soundness examinations (i.e., whether a bank is operating in a sound way). State authorities, in addition to the FDIC, are responsible for overseeing the examination of state non-member banks. : 236 The OCC is the primary regulator for national banks.

Banks and thrift institutions are required to comply with the rules and regulations imposed by each regulatory agency, which each has their own unique set of. In 1979, a formal inter-agency entity known as the Federal Financial Institutions Examination Council (FFIEC) was established with the authority to set consistent principles, standards, and report forms for the purpose of the federal examination of financial institutions. The rules and regulations are always being updated, despite the fact that the FFIEC has led to a greater degree of regulatory consistency among the agencies. Changes in the industry, in addition to alterations in the regulatory framework, have resulted in consolidations within the Federal Reserve, the FDIC, the OTS, and the OCC. There has been a reduction in employees, offices have been shut down, supervisory regions have been combined, and budgets have been slashed. The remaining regulators are facing an increasing strain as a result of an increased workload as well as a rise in the number of banks regulated by each regulator. In the same way that banks are struggling to keep up with the changes in the regulatory environment, regulators are also struggling to efficiently regulate their banks while successfully managing the workload they have. As a result of these developments, banks are receiving less hands-on evaluation by the regulators, the regulators are spending less time with each institution, and there is the possibility for more problems to slip through the cracks. This could potentially result in an overall increase in the number of bank failures across the United States. Because of the low interest rates on loans and the rate competition for deposits, as well as changes in the general market, industry trends, and economic fluctuations, the changing economic environment has a considerable influence on banks and thrifts. These financial institutions struggle to successfully manage their interest rate spread in the face of these challenges. In light of the current state of the economic market, it has been difficult for financial institutions to successfully design their growth strategies. An climate with rising interest rates may appear to be beneficial to financial institutions; nevertheless, the impact of these changes on consumers and companies is difficult to predict, and the struggle for banks to develop while also properly managing the spread in order to earn a return for their shareholders continues to be present. In the current political and economic climate, one of the challenges that still has to be addressed is the management of the asset portfolios held by banks. When the quality of loans begins to be questioned, the very basis upon which a bank is built is jolted, as loans are the primary asset category of a financial institution. Even while this has always been a problem for banks, the deteriorating quality of their assets has become a significant obstacle for financial institutions.

There are various causes for this, one of which is the relaxed attitude that certain banks have developed as a result of the years of "good times." The possibility for this is worsened by the diminution in the regulatory control of banks as well as, in some cases, the depth of management. It is more probable that problems will go unnoticed, which will ultimately result in a substantial impact on the bank when the problems are uncovered. In addition, just like any other type of company, banks try to keep costs down and as a direct result have done away with some expenditures, such as programs that provide sufficient employee training. The banking industry has a plethora of additional issues, one of which is the graying of its ownership groups. The average age of both the management teams and the boards of directors at financial institutions across the country is getting older. In addition, banks are consistently subjected to pressure from shareholders, both public and private, to meet profitability and growth predictions. Banks are under increased pressure from regulators to effectively manage all of the many types of risk. The banking business is another one that features intense levels of competition. The financial services business has seen a proliferation of new participants in recent years, including insurance agencies, credit unions, cheque cashing services, credit card firms, and many more. This has made competition within the market more difficult. In response to this, banks have expanded their operations into the realm of financial instruments by participating in various aspects of the financial market, such as brokerage, and have become significant players in these kinds of endeavors. Another significant obstacle is the aging infrastructure, which is also referred to as legacy IT. Backend systems have been around for decades but are incompatible with modern applications due to their age. Because skilled programmers are becoming increasingly scarce, the cost of fixing faults and building interfaces has skyrocketed.

The lending operations of banks

Banks are required to compete for deposits in order to be in a position to offer home purchasers and builders with the necessary funds. The process of disintermediation led to monies being moved out of savings accounts and into direct market assets like U.S. government bonds. liabilities owed to the Department of Treasury, securities issued by various agencies, and debt owed by corporations. In recent years, one of the most important contributors to the movement of deposits has been the remarkable rise of money market funds. These funds' higher interest rates have been successful in attracting deposits from individual consumers In order to compete for deposits, savings institutions in the United States provide a wide variety of different sorts of programs, including [43]: Accounts in the form of a passbook or those that are simply referred to as deposit accounts allow for the deposit or withdrawal of any amount at any time. NOW and Super NOW accounts are similar to checking accounts in terms of functionality, but they generate interest. There is a possibility that Super NOW accounts will require a minimum balance. Money market accounts come with a cap on the number of preauthorized transfers to other accounts or individuals that can be made each month. These accounts also typically demand a certain minimum or average balance. If you take money from your certificate account before it matures, you risk losing part or all of the interest you earned. Notice accounts are analogous to certificate accounts except that their terms can be indefinitely extended. Participants in a savings program commit to providing the institution with advance notice prior to making a withdrawal. Individual retirement accounts (IRAs) and Keogh plans are two examples of retirement savings vehicles in which both principal contributions and interest earnings are shielded from income taxation until the funds are withdrawn from the account. Checking accounts are provided by some financial organizations in accordance with predetermined guidelines. The person who owns the account has complete control over any and all withdrawals and deposits, as well as the accountability for making such decisions, unless the legal situation calls for a parent or guardian to act otherwise. Club accounts and other types of savings accounts are intended to encourage people to save on a consistent basis in order to accomplish particular objectives.

Different kinds of accounts Branch of a bank in the suburbs

The numerous global accounting standards are applied during the production of bank statements, which are accounting records issued by banks. The generally accepted accounting principles specify two different sorts of accounts: debit and credit. Revenue, Equity, and Liabilities are the three types of credit accounts. Assets and expenses are both considered to be Debit Accounts. A credit account's balance can be increased by the bank by adding a credit, whereas a credit account's balance can be decreased by the bank by adding a debit. When a customer makes a deposit, the customer's savings or bank account in his ledger is debited (and the account is generally in the debit position). On the other hand, when a customer makes a purchase with his credit card, the customer's credit card account in his ledger is credited (and the credit card account is normally in the credit position). When a client examines his or her monthly bank statement, the statement will indicate that deposits have been credited to the account while withdrawals of monies have been debited. On the customer's bank statement, the positive balance will be displayed as a credit balance if the consumer has an overall positive balance. The customer will have a negative amount, which will appear as a debit balance on the bank statement if the customer has an overdrawn account.

Deposits made through a broker

The vast sums of money that deposit brokers send to trust corporations on behalf of their clients serve as one source of deposits for financial institutions like banks. This money will typically move to the financial institutions that provide the most favorable conditions, which are frequently superior to those provided to local depositors. It is conceivable for a bank to conduct operations with no local deposits at all, with the cash coming entirely from deposits brokered by other financial institutions. A bank is placed in a challenging and potentially unsafe position when it accepts a considerable number of such deposits, which are frequently referred to as "hot money." This is because the funds must be lent or invested in a manner that generates a return that is sufficient to pay the high interest that is being offered on the brokered deposits. This could lead to judgments that are high-risk, which could ultimately lead to the bank failing. The average failing bank in the United States during the global financial crisis of 2008 and 2009 had four times the amount of brokered deposits as a percentage of their total deposits compared to failed banks that fell during those same years. These deposits, in conjunction with speculative investments in real estate, were a contributor to the savings and loan crisis that occurred in the 1980s. Banks oppose the regulation of brokered deposits on the grounds that the practice can be a source of external finance to developing areas who have insufficient local deposits. [45] There are several distinct sorts of accounts, including savings, recurrent, and current accounts. Savings accounts are ideal for long-term investments.

Current accounts are ideal for short-term transactions accounts held in custodianship

Accounts that hold assets for the benefit of a third party are referred to as custodial accounts. For instance, businesses that agree to take custody of their customers' cash prior to converting them, returning them, or transferring them might keep those monies in a custodial account with a financial institution.

The phenomenon of globalization in the banking sector

The obstacles to worldwide competition in the banking business have been significantly lowered in recent times because to technological advancements. Increases in telecommunications and other financial technology, such as Bloomberg, have enabled banks to expand their reach all over the world. This is because banks no longer need to be physically close to their customers in order to handle both their financial and risk affairs. The expansion of operations that take place across international borders has led to an increase in the demand for banks that are able to deliver a variety of services to customers of a variety of nationalities. In spite of the lowering of barriers and the increase in operations that span international borders, the banking industry is not even close to being as globalized as some of the other businesses. The Riegle–Neal Act, which encourages more effective banking across state lines, is largely ignored by financial institutions in many countries, including the United States. The market share held by banks that are owned by foreign entities is now less than a tenth of the total market share held by banks operating within a particular nation in the great majority of countries around the world. One of the reasons why the banking industry has not been completely globalized is that it is more easy for small firms and individual borrowers to obtain loans from their neighborhood banks. On the other side, it is not as relevant in what nation the bank is in for huge firms because the financial information of the corporation is available around the globe.

CHAPTER THREE

Banking in India

The beginning of modern banking in India can be traced back to the middle of the 18th century. Both the General Bank of India, which was created in 1786 but collapsed in 1791, and the Bank of Hindustan, which was established in 1770 but went out of business between the years 1829 and 1832, were two of the earliest banks in India. The State Bank of India (SBI) is both the country's most well-known and longest continuously operating financial institution. In the middle of June of 1806, it first opened its doors for business as the Bank of Calcutta. The name was changed to the Bank of Bengal in the year 1809. The other two banks that were established by a presidency government were the Bank of Bombay in 1840 and the Bank of Madras in 1843. This bank was one of the three that were established. In 1921, the three banks came together to form what was then known as the Imperial Bank of India. In 1955, after India gained its independence, the name of the bank was changed to the State Bank of India. Before the Reserve Bank of India was created in 1935, the presidential banks and their successors served in a similar capacity as quasi-central banks. This continued until the Reserve Bank of India was established in 1935 under the Reserve Bank of India Act, 1934. In accordance with the State Bank of India (Subsidiary Banks Act), which was passed in 1959, the State Banks of India were handed control of eight state-associated banks in the year 1960. On the other hand, the merger of these linked banks with SBI took effect on April 1st of this year (2017). The Government of India took over 14 of the country's largest private banks in 1969, and one of those significant financial institutions was the Bank of India. In the year 1980, six further private banks were taken over by the government. [8] Today, the majority of lending in the Indian economy is done by these government-owned banks. Because of their enormous size and extensive network reach, they hold a dominant position in the banking industry. The banking industry in India can be broken down into two basic categories: scheduled and non-scheduled institutions. Those financial institutions that are included in the Reserve Bank of India Act, 1934's 2nd Schedule are referred to as scheduled banks. A further subdivision of the scheduled banks includes nationalized banks, the State Bank of India and its associates, regional rural banks (RRBs), foreign banks, and other Indian private sector banks. [7] On April 1, 2017, the SBI merged its Associate banks into itself to establish the largest bank in India. As a result of this merger, SBI now holds the 236th spot on the Fortune 500 index. When we talk about commercial banks, we're referring to both scheduled and non-scheduled financial institutions that are under the jurisdiction of the Banking Regulation Act of 1949 In general, the supply, product range, and reach of banking in India are fairly mature; despite the fact that reaching the impoverished and rural areas of India is still a difficulty, the supply and product range are fairly mature. The government of India has taken steps to solve this issue, including increasing the branch network of the State Bank of India and providing the National Bank for Agriculture and Rural Development (NABARD) with the ability to provide services such as microfinance. These are two of the efforts that have been established.

The Vedas, which are ancient scriptures from India, make reference to the practice of usury by using the word kusidin, which can be translated as "usurer." The Sutras (written between 700 and 100 BCE) and the Jatakas (written between 600 and 400 BCE) both make reference to usury. Texts written at this time condemned usury; for example, Vasishtha prohibited members of the Brahmin and Kshatriya varnas from engaging in usury. By the second century CE, usury had become increasingly socially acceptable. [11] The Manusmriti considered usury an acceptable means of earning riches or living a livelihood. [12] However, it considered money lending above a particular rate to be a grievous sin. [13] Different ceiling rates applied to different castes. The Jatakas, the Dharmashastras, and Kautilya all make reference to the existence of loan deeds, which are variously referred to as rnapatra, rnapanna, and rnalekhaya. An instrument known as adesha was used later on during the Mauryan period (321–185 BCE). This instrument was an order on a banker directing him to pay the sum on the note to a third party, which is equivalent to the concept of a modern bill of trade. There is evidence to support the claim that these instruments were used extensively [citation required]. Letters of credit were another kind of business communication that was common in larger towns[15].

The Age of the Middle Ages

During the time of the Mughals, loan deeds continued to be used. These documents were known as dastawez (in Urdu and Hindi). There are two distinct kinds of loan deeds that have been documented. The dastawez-e-indultalab was due upon demand, but the dastawez-e-miadi was due after a predetermined amount of time had passed. Barattes, which are payment directives used by royal treasuries, have also been documented in the historical record. There are also records of Indian bankers employing bills of exchange on other countries, which were issued on their behalf. In addition, the development of hundis, a form of credit instrument, took place during this time period and they are still in use today

Colonial time period

During the time that India was under British control, businessmen founded the Union Bank of Calcutta in 1829,[16] at first functioning as a private joint stock organization and then as a partnership. The owners of the Commercial Bank and the Calcutta Bank at the time were also the proprietors of the Union Bank, which was established by mutual agreement as a replacement for the two previous banks. 1840 was the year that it launched an agency in Singapore, and the same year it closed the one that it had opened in Mirzapore the year before. Also in 1840, the Bank disclosed that it had been defrauded by the bank's accountant. The fraud had been perpetrated against the Bank. Despite having been insolvent for some years and having borrowed new money from depositors to pay its dividends, the Union Bank was officially established in 1845 but went bankrupt the following year, in 1848.

The Allahabad Bank is the oldest Joint Stock bank in India; nevertheless, it was not the very first bank in the country when it was founded in 1865 and continues to operate today. This distinction belongs to the Bank of Upper India, which was founded in 1863 and continued to operate until 1913, when it finally went out of business. Prior to its demise, some of the Bank of Upper India's assets and liabilities were transferred to the Alliance Bank of Simla. In the 1860s, foreign banks began to establish themselves in India, particularly in the city of Calcutta. The Comptoir d'Escompte de Paris founded a branch in Calcutta in 1860, and another in Bombay in 1862. Afterwards, branches were established in Madras and Pondicherry, which were both French possessions at the time. In 1864, the first Grindlays Bank branch was established in Calcutta. In the year 1869, the HSBC first opened its doors in Bengal. As a result of Calcutta's status as India's busiest port, which was largely attributable to the commerce of the British Empire, the city eventually developed into a major financial hub. The Oudh Commercial Bank was the very first Indian-owned and operated joint stock bank. It was founded in Faizabad in the year 1881. In 1958, it was a failure. The second bank to open its doors was the Punjab National Bank in 1894 in Lahore. This institution is still operational and has grown to become one of the most important financial institutions in India. Around the turn of the 20th century, the economy of India was going through a period of stability that was relatively favorable. After almost half a century had passed since the Indian uprising, the country's social, industrial, and other infrastructure had significantly improved. Small banks, the majority of which catered to certain racial, ethnic, and religious groupings, had been created by Indians.

There were a few exchange banks and a number of Indian joint stock banks in addition to the presidency banks, which held the majority of the market share in the Indian banking industry. These financial institutions were each active in a distinct sector of the economy. The financing of international trade was the primary focus of the exchange banks, the majority of which were held by Europeans. In general, Indian joint stock banks had insufficient capital, and they lacked the experience and maturity necessary to compete with banks affiliated with the presidency and exchange. As a result of this segmentation, Lord Curzon was able to make the observation that "in respect of banking it seems we are behind the times. We are like some old fashioned sailing ship, divided by solid wooden bulkheads into separate and cumbersome compartments." [citation needed] Lord Curzon was referring to the fact that the financial system in the United Kingdom resembled an antiquated sailing vessel. The Swadeshi movement was the impetus for the founding of a number of financial institutions throughout the years 1906 to 1911. The Swadeshi movement encouraged Indian community members, including local merchants and political figures, to establish banks both for themselves and for their fellow countrymen. The Catholic Syrian Bank, the South Indian Bank, the Bank of India, the Corporation Bank, the Indian Bank, the Bank of Baroda, the Canara Bank, and the Central Bank of India are only few of the banks that were founded at that time and have continued to operate to this day.

The fervor of the Swadeshi movement was responsible for the founding of many private banks in the districts of Dakshina Kannada and Udupi, which had previously been combined under the name South Canara (South Kanara) district. In addition to being the birthplace of a prominent private sector bank, this neighborhood is also home to four nationalized banks. Because of this, the undivided Dakshina Kannada district is referred to as the "Cradle of Indian Banking" The British citizen Sir Osborne Smith served as the first person to hold this position (1 April 1935), while C. D. Deshmukh was appointed as the first Indian governor on August 11, 1943. Shaktikanta Das, who has been serving as the finance secretary for the Government of India, will begin his tenure as the new Governor of the Reserve Bank of India (RBI) on the 12th of December, 2018, taking over for Urjit R. Patel. The period beginning with the First World War (1914–1918) and lasting until the end of the Second World War (1939–1945), as well as the two years that followed, until India attained its independence, were difficult times for Indian banking. In spite of the fact that the Indian economy received an indirect boost as a result of economic operations related to the war, the years of the First World War were chaotic, and it took its toll with banks simply collapsing as a result. According to the data presented in the accompanying table, at least 94 Indian banks went out of business during the years 1913 and 1918.

- *Years Number of institutions*
- *that Authorized Capital attempt was unsuccessful*
- *Capital that has been paid in full*
- *(Thousands of)*
- *1913 12 274 35*
- *1914 42 710 109*
- *1915 11 56 5*

- *1916 13 231 4*

- *1917 9 76 25*

- *1918 7 209 1*

The Years After Independence

Between the years 1938 and 1946, the number of bank branch offices increased to 3,469[19], while deposits more than doubled to reach 962 crore rupees. In spite of this, the partition of India in 1947 had a negative effect on the economies of Punjab and West Bengal, resulting in the suspension of banking operations for several months. The laissez-faire banking system that existed in India came to an end after the country gained its independence. The Government of India took steps to get more involved in the day-to-day operations of the nation's economy, and the Industrial Policy Resolution that was passed by the government in 1948 foresaw the existence of a mixed economic system. As a direct consequence of this, the state became more involved in several facets of the economy, including the banking and financial sectors. The following are the primary actions taken to regulate banking: The Reserve Bank of India, which serves as India's central banking authority, was initially founded in April 1935. However, it was nationalized on January 1, 1949, in accordance with the provisions of the Reserve Bank of India (Transfer to Public Ownership) Act, 1948 (RBI, 2005b). The Banking Regulation Act was passed into law in 1949, and as a result, the Reserve Bank of India (RBI) was given the authority to supervise, manage, and investigate India's financial institutions. In addition, the Banking Regulation Act stated that no new banks or branches of existing banks could be established without first obtaining a license from the Reserve Bank of India (RBI), and that no two institutions could share directors In 1969, there was a nationalization. In spite of the laws, controls, and regulations that are enforced by the Reserve Bank of India, all of the banks in India, with the exception of the State Bank of India (SBI), are still privately owned and run. By the 1960s, the banking industry in India had evolved into a significant component that played a significant role in fostering the growth of the Indian economy. At the same time, it had become a significant employer, and a discussion had begun regarding the possibility of the nationalization of the banking industry. [21] At the time, the Prime Minister of India, Indira Gandhi, presented the intention of the Government of India to the annual conference of the All India Congress Meeting in a paper titled "Stray Thoughts on Bank Nationalization." After that, the government of India passed the Banking Companies (Acquisition and Transfer of Undertakings) Ordinance, 1969, and began the process of nationalizing the country's 14 largest commercial banks at midnight on July 19, 1969. [22] Within two weeks of the issuing of the ordinance, the Parliament enacted the Banking Companies (Acquisition and Transfer of Undertaking) Bill,[24] and it got presidential approval on August 9, 1969. These banks held 85 percent of the country's bank deposits. [22] Within two weeks of the issue of the ordinance, the Parliament passed the Banking Companies (Acquisition and Transfer of Undertaking) Bill.

- *The following financial institutions were taken over by the government in 1969:*

- *Formerly known as the Indian Bank, Allahabad Bank*

65

- *The Baroda State Bank*

- *It's the Bank of India.*

- *This is the Bank of Maharashtra.*

- *The Reserve Bank of India (RBI)*

- *Bank of Canara*

- *Formerly known as the Bank of Baroda, Dena Bank*

- *Bank of the Indians*

- *Bank of Indian Settlements*

- *Bank of the Punjab National*

- *Syndicate Bank, which later became Canara Bank*

- *UCO Bank, Inc.*

- *This is the Union Bank of India.*

- *Formerly known as the United Bank of India and now known as the Punjab National Bank*

- *In 1980, there was a nationalization.*

In 1980, a further six commercial banks were taken over by the government after a second phase of nationalization. One of the stated goals of the nationalization was to provide the government with a greater degree of control over the distribution of credit. Following the second wave of nationalizations, the Indian government gained control of approximately 91 percent of the country's banking sector.

- *In 1980, the following banks were taken over by the government:*

- *Bank of the Punjab and the Sindh*

- *Formerly known as the Bank of Baroda, Vijaya Bank*

- *The Oriental Bank of Commerce, which eventually became the Punjab National Bank*

- *Formerly known as the Union Bank of India, Corporation Bank*

- *Formerly known as the Union Bank of India, Andhra Bank*

- *The New Bank of India, which later became the Punjab National Bank*

Later on, in the year 1993, the government merged New Bank of India with Punjab National Bank. [25] This merger was the only one involving nationally-owned banks at the time, and it brought the total number of nationalized banks down from 20 to 19. Up until the 1990s, the nationalized banks expanded at a rate of approximately 4% per year, which was closer to the average rate of expansion of the Indian economy [citation needed].

The liberalization that took place in the 1990s

Global Trust Bank was the first of such new generation banks to be set up. It later merged with Oriental Bank of Commerce, IndusInd Bank, UTI Bank (since renamed Axis Bank), ICICI Bank, and HDFC Bank. This move – along with the rapid growth in the economy of India – allowed for a small number of private banks to be licensed in the early 1990s. These banks came to be known as New Generation tech-savvy banks. The next stage for the Indian banking industry has been established, and there has been talk of relaxing regulations on foreign direct investment. It is possible for all foreign investors in banks to be granted voting rights that are greater than the current limitation of 10% at this time. [29] In 2019, Bandhan bank expressly upped the foreign investment percentage limit to 49%. [30] It has gone up to 74% with some limits. The banking industry in India was completely upended as a result of the new policy. Bankers were accustomed to operating using a system known as the 4–6–4 method (borrow at 4%, lend at 6%, and go home at 4) until this point in time. The new wave brought with it a modern outlook and ways of working that were more adept with technology for traditional banks. The result of all of this was a boom in retail in India. People asked their banks for more, and in response, they were given more PSB Mergers and Acquisitions During the Decades of the 2000s and 2010s SBI In 2008, State Bank of India combined with its associate bank, State Bank of Saurashtra, and in 2010, State Bank of India merged with State Bank of Indore.The merger of the five remaining associate banks, (namely the State Bank of Bikaner and Jaipur, State Bank of Hyderabad, State Bank of Mysore, State Bank of Patiala, and State Bank of Travancore); and the Bharatiya Mahila Bank) with the SBI was given an in-principle approval by the Union Cabinet on 15 June 2016. [34] This came a month after the SBI board had, on 17 May 2016, cleared a proposal to merge its five associate banks

The Union Cabinet gave its approval for the merger of five affiliate banks with SBI on February 15, 2017. [36] An analyst anticipated an early negative impact due to various pension liability provisions and accounting standards for bad loans. [37][38] The merger became effective on April 1, 2017. On September 17, 2018, the Government of India made a proposal to merge Dena Bank, Vijaya Bank, and the former Bank of Baroda, pending (namesake) consent from the boards of the three banks. [40] On January 2, 2019, the Union Cabinet and the boards of the banks gave their assent to the merger. In accordance with the conditions of the merger, shareholders of Dena Bank and Vijaya Bank got 110 and 402 equity shares of the Bank of Baroda, respectively, each with a face value of 2 for every 1,000 shares that they held in Dena Bank or Vijaya Bank. Beginning on April 1, 2019, the merger was officially put into action. On August 30, 2019, the Finance Minister announced that the Oriental Bank of Commerce and United Bank of India would be merged with Punjab National Bank, making PNB the second largest PSB after SBI with assets of 17.95 lakh crore (US$220 billion) and 11,437 branches. [42][43] MD and CEO of UBI, Ashok Kumar Pradhan, stated that the merged entity would begin functioning from April 1, 2020. [44][45] The Union Cabinet approved the merger on March 4, 2020. The next day, PNB made the announcement that the merger ratios had been accepted by the board of directors. Shareholders of OBC and UBI will each receive 1,150 shares and 121 shares of Punjab National Bank for every 1,000 shares that they own as a result of the merger, which went into effect on April 1, 2020. [46] The merger was completed on April 1, 2020. Following the merger, Punjab National Bank has risen to the position of being India's second-largest public sector bank .

Bank of Canara

Canara Bank and Syndicate Bank are going to combine their operations, as was stated by the Finance Minister on the 30th of August, 2019. The proposal will result in the creation of the fourth largest PSB after SBI, PNB, and BoB, with assets valued at 15.20 lakh crore (US$190 billion) and 10,324 branches. [48][43] The merger was approved by the Board of Directors of Canara Bank on September 13, 2019, and by the Union Cabinet on March 4, 2020. Canara Bank took control of Syndicate Bank on April 1, 2020, and shareholders of Syndicate Bank were given 158 equity shares in Canara Bank for every 1,000 shares they owned.

This is the Union Bank of India.

The announcement that Andhra Bank and Corporation Bank would be combined into Union Bank of India was made on the 30th of August, 2019, by the Finance Minister. The proposal would make Union Bank of India the fifth largest PSB in India, with assets worth 14.59 lakh crore (US$180 billion) and 9,609 branches. [52][43] The merger was approved by the Board of Directors of Andhra Bank on September 13. The Union

Cabinet approved the merger on March 4, and it was completed on April 1, 2020. [46]

Bank of the Indians

The merger between Indian Bank and Allahabad Bank was officially announced on the 30th of August, 2019, by the Finance Minister. The Union Cabinet gave its approval to the merger on March 4, 2020, making it official. The proposal would result in the creation of the sixth largest PSB in the country, with assets totaling 8.08 lakh crore (US$100 billion). On the first of April in the year 2020, Indian Bank took possession of Allahabad Bank. In the 2020s, efforts will be made to save both commercial and cooperative banks. The "Yes" bank In April of 2020, the Reserve Bank of India (RBI) enlisted the services of the State Bank of India (SBI) to assist in the rescue of the ailing lender Yes Bank. This was done in the form of an investment, and it received assistance from a number of other lenders, including ICICI Bank, HDFC Bank, and Kotak Mahindra Bank. SBI eventually owned 48% of the share capital of Yes bank, but in the months that followed, it participated in an FPO that reduced its stake to 30%.

This is the Lakshmi Vilas Bank.

Following poor management and two unsuccessful efforts to combine with NBFCs, the Reserve Bank of India (RBI) requested that DBS Bank India Limited (DBIL) take over the operations of the private sector bank

Lakshmi Vilas Bank in November of 2020. This was because the bank's net value had turned negative. DBS India, which only had 12 branches at the time, benefited from LVB's network of 559 branches. As a first of its type action, the Reserve Bank of India (RBI) has requested that holders of Tier-II bonds write off their holdings in LVB.

Co-operative Bank of Punjab and Maharashtra (PMCB)

In January 2022, the Reserve Bank of India (RBI) requested that Unity Small Finance Bank Limited (Unity SFB) take over the operations of the private sector bank Punjab and Maharashtra Co-operative Bank (PMC). This request came in the wake of mismanagement and an unsuccessful attempt to merge with NBFCs or SFBs. Centrum Finance and BharatPe, a supplier of payment services, were at the time in the process of establishing Unity SFB with the intention of absorbing the liabilities of the scam-affected bank. The Reserve Bank of India (RBI) took an unprecedented step when it approved the merger of an existing cooperative bank with an SFB that was in the process of being constituted at the time.

Reorganization of the regional rural banks

In late 2010, a new strategy was implemented that resulted in the RRBs serving a smaller locality that encompassed a few districts being combined into an institution that operated at the state level. This was done in response to the merger of nationalized banks and the subsequent increase in those banks' stock in RRBs. RRBs were basically transformed into a subsidiary bank of the promoter nationalized bank with state equity, which led to the elimination of the existential competition and collaboration that existed amongst RRBs.

The present time period

The banking industry in India can be broken down into two primary categories: scheduled banks and non-scheduled banks. Scheduled Banks consist of all financial institutions that are listed in the Reserve Bank of India Act, 1934's Second Schedule. Both Scheduled Commercial Banks and Scheduled Co-operative Banks are included in this group of financial institutions. Both urban and state cooperative banks are included in the category of scheduled cooperative banks.

- *IDBI Bank Ltd. is considered to be a part of the other public sector bank category within the framework of the bank group-wise classification.*

- *The Expanding Role of Scheduled Commercial Banks in the Indian Financial System*

- *Indicators as of the 31st of March*

- *2005 2006 2007 2008 2009 2010 2011 2012 2013*

- *There are a total of 284 218 178 169 166 163 163 169 151 commercial banks in the world.*

- *There are a total of 70,373, 72,072, 74,653, 78,787, 82,897, 88,203, 94,019, 102,377, and 109,811 branches.*

- *Population distributed across each bank, in thousands: 16 16 15 15 15 14 13 13 12*

Aggregate Deposits $17,002 billion (US$210 billion), $21,090 billion (US$260 billion), $26,119 billion (US$330 billion), $31,969 billion (US$400 billion), $38,341 billion (US$480 billion), $44,928 billion (US$560 billion), $52,078 billion (US$650 billion), $59,091 billion (US$740 billion), and $67,504.54 billion (US$850 billion). Credit Extended by Banks 11,004 billion yen (US$140 billion) 15,071 billion yen (US$190 billion) 19,312 billion yen (US$240 billion) 23,619 billion yen (US$300 billion) 27,755 billion yen (US$350 billion) 32,448 billion yen (US$410 billion) 39,421 billion yen (US$490 billion) 46,119 billion yen (US$580 billion) The deposit, expressed as a percentage of GNP (at factor cost), is as follows: 62% 64% 69% 73% 77% 78% 78% 78% 78% 79% Deposits per person range from: 16,281 (US$200) to 19,130 (US$240) to 23,382 (US$290) to 28,610 (US$360) to 33,919 (US$420) to 39,107 (US$490) to 45,505 (US$570) to 50,183 (US$630) to 56,380 (US$710) Credit per capita of 10,752 ($130), 13,869 ($170), 17,541 ($220), 21,218 ($270), 24,617 ($310), 28,431 ($360), 34,187 ($430), 38,874 ($490), and 44,028 ($550).Credit Deposit Ratio 63% 70% 74% 75% 74% 74% 74% 75% 74% 74% 74% 76% 79% 79% As a result of the fact that it is anticipated that growth in the Indian economy will be robust for a considerable amount of time, particularly in its services sector, there is anticipated to be an increase in the demand for banking services, particularly retail banking, mortgages, and investment services. Additionally, one should anticipate mergers and acquisitions, takeovers, and asset sales.

Warburg Pincus was granted permission in March 2006 by the Reserve Bank of India to grow its holding in Kotak Mahindra Bank, which is a private sector bank, to 10%. Since the Reserve Bank of India (RBI) set regulations in 2005 requiring that any holding above 5% in the private sector banks would need to be vetted by them, this was the first time that an investor was permitted to own more than 5% in a private sector bank. This was also the first time that an investor was allowed to hold more than 5% in a public sector bank In recent years, opponents have asserted that non-government owned banks are overly aggressive in their attempts to collect loans in the areas of housing, automobiles, and personal loans. There have been reports in the media that the banks' efforts to recover defaulted loans have caused some of the debtors to take their own lives.[57][58][59] By 2013, the Indian Banking Industry had an aggregate deposit of 67,504.54 billion (US$850 billion or €830 billion) and bank credit of 52,604.59 billion (US$660 billion or €640 billion). Additionally, the Indian Banking Industry had a total of 109,811 branches in India and 171 branches abroad. In comparison, the total revenue generated by India's commercial banks was 9,148.59 billion rupees (about US$110 billion or €110 billion) for the financial year 2012–13, which resulted in a net profit of 1,027.51 billion rupees (about US$13 billion or €13 billion). Prime Minister's People Money Scheme is the English translation of the Hindi phrase "Pradhan Mantri Jan Dhan Yojana," which translates to "Prime Minister's People Money Scheme." [60] On the day of the scheme's inauguration, 1.5 Crore (15 million) bank accounts were opened under this scheme. [61][62] As of the 15th of July, 2015, 16.92 crore (169.2 million) accounts had been opened, with approximately 2 trillion (or approximately $2 trillion) in

Transaction Banks

The Reserve Bank of India (RBI) came up with the idea for a brand-new type of banking institution called a payments bank. These banks are able to accept a restricted deposit, but the amount that each consumer can deposit is now capped at 2 lakh. These financial institutions might not give out loans or credit cards, but they could provide checking and savings accounts instead. It's possible for payment banks to issue ATM and debit cards, in addition to providing internet banking and mobile banking services. On July 17, 2014, the draft guidelines for licensing payments banks in the private sector were developed and made available for public comment. [64] The banks will be licensed as payments banks in accordance with Section 22 of the Banking Regulation Act, 1949, and will be registered as public limited companies in accordance with the Companies Act, 2013. [65]

Small financial institutions

The Reserve Bank of India (RBI) approved the establishment of ten small finance banks in 2016, with the intention of advancing the goal of expanding access to financial services. Since that time, all 10 of them have been granted the required licenses. A small finance bank is a specialized kind of bank that caters to the requirements of customers who, in the past, have not utilized the services of scheduled banks. Each of these financial institutions is required to establish at least 25 percent of their branches in regions that are unserved by any other financial institutions (termed "unbanked regions"). A small finance bank should hold 75% of its net credits in loans to enterprises in priority sector lending, and 50% of the loans in its portfolio must be less than 25 lakh (US$34,000) [66]. A small finance bank should hold 75% of its net credits in loans to firms in priority sector lending.

Codes and standards for the banking industry

The Banking codes and standards Board of India is the primary topic of The Banking Codes and Standards Board of India is an independent and autonomous banking industry group that monitors banks in India. S. S. Tarapore, a former deputy governor of the Reserve Bank of India, came up with the concept to organize this committee in order to improve the quality of banking services available in India.

Data Security Flaws data breach in 2016 affecting Indian banks

In October of 2016, it was announced that numerous Indian banks had suffered a massive data breach involving debit cards. According to estimates, the security of 3.2 million debit cards was breached. SBI, HDFC Bank, ICICI, Yes Bank, and Axis Bank were among the most severely affected major Indian banks. [67] A large number of cardholders claimed that their cards had been used fraudulently in China. Because of this, India's banking industry experienced one of the largest card replacement drives in its history. The State Bank of India, the country's largest financial institution, has declared that it will cancel and replace over 600,000 debit cards.

Summary

The first prototypical banks of merchants of the ancient world are where the history of banking gets its start.globe that provided grain loans to farmers and merchants transporting goods from city to city; reported ashaving taken place around the year 2000 B.C. in the regions of Assyria and Japonia, respectively. In later years, whenLenders with their offices in temples were active in ancient Greece and across the Roman Empire.added not one but two significant new features: the capacity to take deposits and the ability to exchange currency.Archaeological findings from this time period in ancient China and India point to the existence of monetary systems at the time.the practice of lending.The origins of banking as we understand it now can be traced back to the middle ages and the early Renaissance.Italy, specifically to the prosperous towns located in the north such as Florence, Venice, and Genoa. The Bardi and Peruzzi Fashion Houses Families controlled the financial system in Florence during the 14th century and established branches in nu-

merous other cities.regions within Europe.The growth of banking eventually reached Europe as well, when a number of significant banks were established.The city of Amsterdam was a hotbed of innovation during the 16th century, particularly during the time of the Dutch Republic.

During the 17th century in London. During the 20th century, advancements were made in various forms of communication. Modern computing led to significant shifts in the manner that banks performed their operations and enabled them toexponential growth in terms of both size and global distribution. The financial crisis that began in the late 2000s sawfailure of a considerable number of banks, including some of the largest banks in the world, as well as many smaller banks.discussion regarding the regulation of banks.The very first examples of bankingThere is a strong connection between the development of banking and the evolution of currency, but banking transactionspresumably date back to a time before the creation of money. The deposits were initially composed of grain and then expanded to include otherproducts such as animals, agricultural implements, and, in the long run, precious metals such as gold,in the shape of compact plates that are simple to transport.In the eras preceding the widespread adoption of Christianity, the people's economic lives were characterized by aflowed around the homes of the Familia Regala and its clergy, which served as the primary locations for maintaining security.provided for the primary purpose of the storage and distribution of crops. Therefore, the buildings that were utilizedpalaces and temples, which were supported primarily by this elite, became the setting of the earliest social gatherings.trade that shares some similarities with the financial practices that are prevalent in modern civilization, in which theIt was guaranteed that the wealth of society would be preserved. The most secure locations were palaces and temples.places to store gold as well since they were regularly staffed and of high quality construction.The first financial institutions were known as "merchant banks," and they were established somewhere during the Middle Ages.Italian businessmen who dealt in grain. As a result of the Lombardy merchants and bankers' increasing prominence as a result of thecereal crops doing well in the Lombardplains, a large number of Jewish refugees seeking refuge from Spanish persecutionwere drawn to participate in the trade.

They carried with them time-honored customs from both the Middle East and the Far East.East routes of the silk trade. These strategies were at one time designed to provide financial support for lengthy commercial journeys.were used as a source of funding for the production and commerce surrounding grain.Because Jews were unable to legally own land in Italy, they moved their businesses into the thriving marketplaces and halls ofLombardy, together with the local merchants, and put up their benches to engage in the trading of crops. They held it.one significant benefit that they have over the natives. Usury was a sin that Christians were strongly forbidden from committing.characterized as lending money at a high interest rate (the practice of usury is strongly condemned in Islam). The Jewish peopleOn the other side, entrants to the market could make high-risk loans to farmers based on the crops they now have in the field.loan at interest rates that, according to the teachings *of the Church, would have been considered usurious; however, the Jews were not.subject to the instructions of the Church. They would therefore be able to protect their rights to the selling of grain against thethe harvest in the end. After that, they started making payments in advance against the grain that would be delivered in the future.transported to a great distance of ports. In both instances, they were able to make a profit by leveraging the existing discount against the original price.the price in the future. This two-handed trade required a lot of time, which led to the development of a class ofthose merchants who were dealing in grain debt rather than grain itself.The Jewish businessman was responsible for both the finance (credit) and underwriting (insurance) of the company.At the beginning of the growing season, financing was provided in the form of a crop loan, which enabled for the successful harvest.a farmer in order for him to create and produce (via sowing, growing, weeding, and harvesting) his own product.crop harvested once a year. Crop insurance, often known as commodity insurance, was the kind of underwriting that guaranteed theshipment of the harvest to the purchaser, who is often a merchant or wholesaler. In addition, market participantscarried out the duties of a merchant by arranging for supplies to be delivered to the purchaser of the harvest.*

in the event that crop failure occurs, through alternative sources, such as grain stockpiles or alternative marketplaces, for exampl e.failing to succeed. Additionally, he had the ability to "keep the farmer (or other commodity producer) in business during a time of difficulty."crop (or commodity) insurance protects farmers against financial loss in the event of crop failure due to factors such as drought.against the possibility that his crop will not be successful.The practice of merchant banking evolved from the financing of trade on one's own behalf to the settlement of deals for other parties.the others, and later on to the practice of retaining deposits for the settlement of "billette" or notes made by the people.who were still involved in actually brokering the grain. Because of this, the term "bank" originally referred to the "benches" of merchants. from the Italian word for bench, banca (which is derived from the same word as a counter), the large grain markets developed into centersfor the purpose of keeping money in exchange for a bill (also known as a billlette, a note, a letter of formal exchange, and later a bill of exchange).These money were initially deposited in the form of a check, followed by an exchange, and eventually became a check.settlement of grain trades, but in the meanwhile, they were frequently utilized for the bench's own trading activities.The word "bankrupt" is a corruption of the Italian word "bancarotta," which literally translates to "broken bench."occurred as a result of anyone losing his traders' deposits. Being "broke" carries the same connotation as being "poor."By the late 16th century and throughout the 17th century, the conventional banking tasks ofThe services of accepting deposits, lending money, exchanging money, and moving monies were all rolled into one.through the issuing of bank debt that acted as a replacement for precious metal coinage such as gold and silver.By creating a secure and stable economic environment, innovative banking practices encouraged the expansion of commercial and industrial sectors.a money supply that is more responsive to commercial needs, as well as convenient ways of payment, as well asas well as by "discounting" the amount of the company's debt. By the close of the 17th century, banking had also become an establishedassuming increasing significance in light of the finance needs of the relatively recent and aggressiveEuropean nations and states. This would eventually result in governmental controls as well as the establishment of the first central banks.The flourishing of innovative banking strategies and procedures in Amsterdam, in addition to the city's overall success,trading city of Antwerp contributed to the dissemination of ideas and ideals to London and assisted in thedevelopments occurring in various other parts of Europe.The deregulation and globalization of the 1980sThe deregulation of financial markets in the 1980s led to a proliferation of global banking and capital market services.markets for trading financial instruments in a number of countries. The 'Big Bang' that took place in London in 1986 and allowed banks toaccess new forms of capital markets, which led to significant changes in the way that banks operate.

functioned as well as gained access to financing. Additionally, it was the beginning of a trend in which retail banks began to purchaseThe creation of universal banks by investment banks and stock brokers, which provided a diverse array of financial servicesProviders of banking services. After much of the Glass-Steagall Act was repealed, the practice also expanded to the United States.This allowed US retail banks to engage in large rounds of mergers and acquisitions once the law was removed in the 1980s.acquisitions as well as other investment banking activity are something we engage in.As a direct consequence of a significant increase in demand, financial services continued their rapid expansion throughout the 1980s and 1990s.because to factors including, but not limited to, an increase in demand from businesses, governments, and financial institutionsThe conditions in the financial markets were upbeat and, generally speaking, positive. The interest rates offered byThe United States saw a drop of approximately 15% for the previous two years. Treasury notes to around 5% throughout the time periodthe 20-year period, during which time financial assets rose at a rate that was roughly twice as fast as the rate at which thethe economy of the world. During this time period, there was a notable increase in the globalization of financial markets. TheDuring the first decade of the 21st century, the process of financial innovation made significant strides forward.boosting the relevance of nonbank financial institutions while also improving their profitability. That profitability in the first placeconfined to sectors other than banking, the Office of the Comptroller of the Currency (OCC) has been prompted toCurrency (OCC) in order to incentivize banks to investigate various different financial instruments and diversify their holdingsbanks' businesses while also enhancing the overall economic well-being of banks. Therefore, in light of the separateBoth the banking industry and the non-banking sector are researching and implementing new financial products.There is a gradual blurring of the lines between the various types of financial institutions as the industry continues to consolidate.

Conclusion

The first decade of the 21st century was also the decade that saw the pinnacle of technological advancement inbanking throughout the course of the past thirty years and witnessed a significant transition away from traditional banking tothe internet.The Development of Banking Services and the Country's Rich History in IndiaThe history of banking in India goes back a very long time. There is literature that dates back to the Vedic period that records thelending money to people that need it. Lending money was considered to be identical with banking. Manusmrithi, also known asincludes discussion of loans, interest rate, deposits, and pledges. At this rate, legal interest charges could be levied.between two and five percent each month depending on your position in the hierarchy. The highest possible rate of interest.The State established the minimum amount that is recoverable on the principle. It was forbidden to engage in usury. Reimbursement forThe deceased person's heir was required to fulfill their moral commitment to repay the loan. Because of the expansion of both trade andConsequently, the business community quickly developed a method of money transfer that could be used everywhere.the nation.The development of the British Empire in India marked the beginning of the modern banking system in that country. The British strengthened their position.after defeating Tipu Sultan in battle, they were able to consolidate their authority and become the most powerful force in India.1799 saw the battle of Srirangapattanam take place. The ambitious drive for power on the part of Lord Mornington (LaterThe Marquis of Welle, Sly). The decision made at the time by the Governor General of Fort William in Bengal resulted to asevere depletion of the East India Company's resources, which ultimately resulted in the company's collapse.establishing the Bank of Calcutta in 1806 as a means of collecting funds. The circumstances that were present at the timeThe writings of a few Britishers, like C.N. Cooke, Deputy Secretary and others, provided a means of determining time. It was declared by the Treasurer of the Bank of Bengal in his book "Banking in India" that usury is unethical.

during the nineteenth century, prevailed in India to a greater extent than in any other country. The currency of the country.The interest rates on loans given to the farmers by the lender ranged from 40 to 50 to 60 percent. The European community has reached an impasse.comparatively in a better position. He explained the extremely high rates by pointing to the precarious nature of many of the credit options.as well as the challenges involved in making them a reality. The Indian merchants very frequently played the role of lender to theEuropean merchants who were offered an in-

terest rate that was lower than the going market rate.Prior to the establishment of the three Presidency Banks, the European Agency Houses fulfilled the function of The banking industry. They accepted deposits from Europeans who were traveling through India as well as British Officers who were posted in India.had completed their military service in India and relocated to Europe. They used finances such as this to finance commerce, and at There were moments when it was even beneficial to the government. There was a credit network that worked extremely well for flow.transfer of funds from one region to another inside India that is made possible by the various Indian banking companies.As the Agency Houses gained more wealth, they became interested in running banks as well. Both Alexander andIn the 1770s, the Company, then a prominent Agency House, took over management of the Bank of Hindustan. TheIt is unknown when exactly that bank opened its doors for business. There is the Bengal Bank, as well as the General Bank.of India were also begun in the eighteenth century by other Agency Houses in Bengal. These houses were located in Bengal. In1819 saw the establishment of the Commercial Bank, and the following year saw the establishment of the Calcutta Bank by the Agency.The homes. None of these banks had limited liability, and none of them were even close to being considered joint stock banks.They were partnerships that carried an unlimited level of responsibility. The idea of limited responsibility did not exist at the time.before the 1860 Companies Act was published in the official statute books. Up to that point, banks were required to either obtaina unique Charter from the Crown in order to operate, or *else they were required to do so with limitless liability.The Bank of Bengal may trace its roots back to the Bank of Calcutta, which was established in 1806. 1862 was the year when theThe Presidency Banks lost their right to issue currency in the form of notes. Additionally, the Governmentretracted their nominations for positions on their Board of Directors. On the other hand, they were granted the opportunityin charge of the administration of the Treasury of the Government in each of the Presidency Towns and each of their respective branches.The Bank of Bombay failed in 1867, and its assets were voluntarily liquidated early the following year, in 1868.It was finally put out of business in 1872, but the bank was able to satisfy its obligation to thethe general population.In the years that followed, in 1867, a new bank that would come to be known as the New Bank of Bombay was established in order tostart conducting business as a bank. In 1876, legislation known as the Presidency Banks Act was enacted in order toin order to enable the government to regulate the banks, there should be a single law that applies to all three of them.the operation of these banking institutions. Earlier, the government divested itself of its interest in the company.the three banks in question.The Swadeshi Movement, which encouraged people in India to establish a large number of new organizations, includedacted as a catalyst for the establishment of new starling banks. The number of banks organized as joint stock companies rose.to a remarkable degree throughout the boom years of 1906 to 1913. The People's Bank of India Ltd., The Bank of India, and other Indian financial institutionsIt was at this time that the Central Bank of India, Indian Bank Ltd., and* the Bank of Baroda were established.the end. This boom lasted until it was replaced by the slump that occurred from 1913 to 1917, which was the first crisis thatthe difficulties that the Indian joint stock banks faced.In 1921, the three Presidency Banks located in Calcutta, Bombay, and Madras were consolidated into one institution known as the.Through the passage of the Imperial Bank of India Act in 1920, the Imperial Bank was established.

This bank did not have any net assets.the ability to issue bank notes, but was allowed to oversee the clearing house and maintain some of the reserves instead.budgetary gaps in the government. The Reserve Bank of India came into being with the passage of the Reserve Bank of India Act of 1934.The Reserve Bank of India was established so that it could fulfill the role of Central Bank. It was able to obtain the permission toIn place of the Imperial Bank, the National Bank of Canada was authorized to issue notes and served as the banker to the government.On the other hand, the Imperial Bank was granted the authority to perform the duties of the Reserve Bank of Australia.India in locations in which the Reserve Bank did not have any branches.The Imperial Bank was acquired, and the State Bank of India was established as a result of the passage of the State Bank of India Act in 195 5.assets transferred to a brand-new financial institution known as the State Bank of India. The Reserve Bank was established in 1874 as ashareholders' financial institution. The Reserve Bank Amendment Act of 1948 led to its eventual nationalization.as a direct result of the nationalization of the Bank of England in the year 1946.The Nationalization of BanksAfter the country's *independence, the most important historical event in the history of banking in India isunquestionably the nationalization of fourteen of the country's largest banks on July 19, 1969; the implementation ofIn the beginning of 1969, the government thought that social control over banks was unsuccessful and subsequently abandoned the effort.that India's commercial banks did not boost the amount of money they lent to the country's core industries suchNationalization was seen as an important step toward attaining goals related to agriculture, small-scale industries, and other areas.the pattern of socialism that prevails throughout society. The government-owned banks were supposed to increase their lending to disadvantaged areas.significance to the government and the use of their resources for the benefit of the general populace. Aa plan that went awry, including objectives, rules, management, and other topics, was drafted for these banks.1980 saw the nationalization of six additional banks from the private sector, expanding the scope of the public domain.over the financial area of banking.It was an understanding of the potential of the banking system to facilitate broader economic growth that led to nationalization.goals related to the economy. The banks were required to broaden their reach and grow their network in order for theIt was decided to place more emphasis on the idea of mass banking rather than class banking. Increasing availability of credit inThe rural area was one of the most important goals.Indeed, the advantages brought about by nationalization have been rather remarkable. The extensive branching pattern of thesePractically every part of the country, especially rural and formerly undeveloped areas, now has at least* one bank branch.places that are not banked. In June of 1969, there were 8262 branches in the branch network. Today, there are over 60000 branches.by 1992, with a significant increase (80%) in the number of people living in rural areas. The typical quantity of individuals satisfiedby means of a branch, the number was reduced from over 60,000 to 11,000. The distribution of credit is taking place throughout a wider scope.disseminated out across the entire country as opposed to being concentrated mainly in the developed states. The total amount of deposits in 1969 wasto 30% of G.D.P. and then goes up to 10% after that. By 1990, advances had grown to 25% while deposits had grown to 30%.that G.D.P. The proportion of deposits coming from rural areas increased from three percent to fifteen percent, which led to aa greater concentration of efforts directed on the collection of resources from rural areas. The total amount of deposits increased from Rs.4669 crores in July of 1969, compared to 2,75,000 crores on March 31st, 1993. Forty percent of the total credit was awarded togeared at the most important industries.

The organization utilized more than 45 percent of the total deposits.government to support its goals for the next five years. However, this expansion did not occur without a corresponding increase in expenses. The financial system as a whole has also expa nded.customer service has degraded as a result of growing costs and inadequate staffing levels due to huge and unmanageableefficiency in work. The directed credit scheme has resulted in significant missed payments, which have an effect on the verythe economic health of the banking system.There is a Wide Variety of Banking

ServicesThe various varieties of banking services are depicted in the flowchart that may be found below.1. Services Provided by the Central Bank2. Services Provided by Commercial Banks3. Personalized Financial and Banking Services4. financial services that are not provided by banks;1. Services Provided by Central Banks: The Central Bank of any Country

(i) Prints and Distributes Currency and Bank Notesnotes;

(ii) performs the duties associated with the government treasury; and

(iii) is responsible for the management of the country's finances. the affairs of the nation, supervises both the internal and external value of money, and

(iv) acts as the nation's chief executive officer.bank of the Government and, last but not least, functions as a bank for banks and other financial institutions.2. Services offered by commercial banks These commercial banking services include, among other things:

(i) receivinga variety of deposit forms;

the provision of a range of loan types; the provision of a selection of non-banking services.customer services such as the provision of lockers and assistance with the direct payment of rent for housing accommodationsthe monthly electricity payment, as well as share-calls. money, the insurance premium, or something similar. Additionally a commercial bankprovides advice on the allocation, reinvestment, or transfer of funds related to investments.3. The establishment of specialized banking institutions as well as the provision of specialized banking services.specialized banking services, such as those offered by industrial banks, in order to furnish busi-

nesses with long-term credit and working capital; loans granted by land mortgage banks based on equitable mortgages; rural credit-Banks with the purpose of producing capital in order to issue rural credit; developmental banks to support any and all rural activities geared for personal growth. These kinds of financial institutions take deposits of any kind but put the funds to use.amount in the region that it focuses on specifically.4. Financial Services That Are Not Provided by Banks There are a Wide Variety of Institutions That Do Not Provide Banking Services.Providers of financial services. Mutual funds are organizations that pool the financial resources of their members.as well as investing in the long-term capital of enterprises, either directly in the primary market or indirectly through secondary marketsindirect participation in the financial market. The compensation that financial organizations that act as portfolio managers getmanaging the public's money as well as the money deposited with it for the benefit of or on behalf of the depositors. The portfolio in questionThe job of managing the funds belonging to the principal is taken on by the managers.pro duce the highest possible profit.

Milton Keynes UK
Ingram Content Group UK Ltd.
UKHW020929231123
433129UK00016B/872